C000186748

The Greatest Guide to

Walking & Mountain Hiking

This is a **GREATEST**GUIDES title

Greatest Guides Limited, Woodstock, Bridge End, Warwick CV34 6PD, United Kingdom

www.greatestguides.com

Series created by Harshad Kotecha

Greatest Guides is committed to a sustainable future for our planet. This book is printed on paper certified by the Forest Stewardship Council.

MIX
Paper
FSC FSC® C020837

Printed and bound in the United Kingdom

ISBN 978-1-907906-12-1

This book is dedicated to
Jackie Leigh and Albert Procter

Contents

“Of all excercises walking is the best.”

Thomas Jefferson
US President (1801—1809)

A few words from Mark…

I remember the day that I got hooked on walking. My friend had persuaded me to climb *Black Hill* in the Derbyshire Peak District with her. As soon as we set off, I realised just how unfit I was and spent the next hour regretting it. I struggled to keep up. She strode purposefully up the hillside, laughing and chatting, whilst I gasped for air and felt nauseous. I longed to stop and turn around but had to go on – I couldn't lose face by turning back. The ordeal continued.

Things soon changed, once we reached the muddy summit. I quickly recovered and felt euphoric that I had reached the top. Suddenly it felt amazing. The views were like nothing I had seen before and I was captivated by the wild feel of the place. I tucked into the sandwich I had brought with me, and decided that I was going to do a lot more walking in the future.

That was the start of my walking adventures. Walking became an important part of my life and took me to new places. Along the way, I explored most of the UK's popular walking areas and trekked and climbed mountains around the world. I even moved house to be closer to my favourite walking location.

Putting on my boots and going for a walk has never lost its appeal. I hope this book encourages you to become a regular walker too. I know walking will enrich your life.

Mark

Walk the Walk

“Walking is man’s best medicine.”

Hippocrates
Greek physician (460 BC—377 BC)

Chapter 1

Walk the Walk

It's good for you!

Going for a walk is one of those simple pleasures in life that makes you feel good on the inside, and, if you do it regularly enough, look better on the outside too. A walk liberates you from the confines of your home and car, and gets you into the great outdoors. It's a wonderful excuse to get away from it all, get fit, de-stress, and experience new places. Oh, and get lots of lovely fresh air.

A picture of health

These days we tend to travel even the shortest distance by car; we work in non-physical employment, then we go home and sprawl for hours in front of the television. But, when exercise is lacking from our lives, problems can occur. Physical inactivity is blamed for obesity and it contributes to a number of illnesses and medical conditions. Doctors agree that we can all benefit from some exercise. The good news is that walking regularly helps you keep fit and healthy.

FASCINATING FACT

Regular walking can halve your risk of heart attack.

Brain food

Just in case you need more reasons to walk regularly, there are others. Walking isn't just good for your physical health; it promotes mental well-being too. It reduces anxiety and stress, and aids restful sleep. Research shows that spending time in an outdoor environment has a positive affect on your mental health. If you want to chill out – go for a walk.

The body produces serotonin after exercise, making you feel more energetic and cheerful. Regular walking counteracts the lower serotonin levels associated with depression, anxiety and aggression. Exercise also releases endorphins, a natural painkiller, which give some people a 'high' afterwards. Now you know why walkers have always got smiles on their faces.

Make friends

Walking is a way to meet new people and make new friends. Join a walking club to meet like-minded individuals. Club walking trips are an excellent opportunity to chat to and get to know people. People you meet whilst walking can become friends for life.

The Ramblers Association is an organisation that brings together people with an interest in walking. They have walking groups based throughout the UK, which organise regular walking trips for its members. A number of commercial organisations also run walking weekends and holidays. You will see them advertising in walking magazines, the travel sections of newspapers, and on the internet. If you are looking for love, you can find dating agencies for walkers and outdoor enthusiasts!

Of all exercises walking is the best

There are lots of health benefits from regular walking:

- Improves your heart and circulation.
- Lowers blood pressure and cholesterol levels.
- Promotes weight loss.
- Improves flexibility of joints and muscles.
- Builds strength in muscles and bones.
- Boosts your immune system.
- Helps you breathe more efficiently.

Regular walking also reduces the risk of a number of health problems occurring, including:

- Coronary heart disease.
- Strokes.
- Diabetes.
- High blood pressure.
- Bowel cancer.
- Alzheimer's disease.
- Arthritis.

(Source: Bird and Reynolds 2001, Walking the Way to Health – this is a joint initiative between Natural England and the British Heart Foundation.)

TOP T!P

See your doctor for a medical check-up before embarking on any new fitness program, particularly if you are overweight, haven't exercised in a long time, or suffer from a medical condition.

Groupie or lone ranger?

Groups – Walking with others is a fabulous way to share the outdoor experience, and part of the fun is reliving the day's happenings over a drink or meal afterwards. Being part of a group lets the novice walker enjoy the outing without being concerned with reading maps and navigating. It's also reassuring to know that there are others around to help out, in case of difficulty.

Going solo – Solo walking has its own rewards. Going solo lets you make your own decisions and travel at your own pace. Being 'alone' provides you with some solitude in today's hectic times. It is a peaceful and liberating experience. Perfect if you don't feel sociable and want to escape for a while. It's a chance to think and to work out problems. Many of life's dilemmas can be solved during a good walk.

Fashion victim?

Outdoor wear isn't cheap. Branded outdoor wear has become very fashionable. Colours and styles change with the seasons nowadays, and we now have the equivalent of designer labels for outdoor enthusiasts.

Price – Price often reflects quality. 'Technical' clothing and equipment makes use of special materials and has undergone extensive research and development by manufacturers. These items tend to be more hardwearing and better suited to challenging outdoor environments. So expect to pay premium prices for these.

Save money – Can you go walking without breaking the bank? Yes, absolutely. Look for lesser-known brands that use similar materials; buy

your gear in end-of-season sales; and remember to suggest, helpfully, 'walking gear' when asked what you want for your birthday and Christmas presents.

Squeeze it in

You can squeeze walks into the busiest of schedules. Even a little goes a long way to improving your well-being. The shortest stroll through a bluebell wood lifts your spirits on the gloomiest of days; lunchtime walks provide a stress-free zone away from the pressures of work, and weekend walking trips are an opportunity to escape and discover new places.

With our modern-day, sedentary lifestyles, finding time for exercise has become even more important. Walking is an enjoyable way to get fit, without the need to enrol at the local gym and dress in Lycra. There's no excuse for not getting into the 'green gym' of the great outdoors. So head out there and get walking!

Take your dog – if you have one

Dog walking duties needn't feel like a chore when you take your dog walking with you. Dog walking is easier when your dog accompanies you, on your walk. You both enjoy the exercise together. They provide companionship when you don't want to walk alone, and they make you feel safer when you venture into remote areas.

To ensure that walking with your dog is enjoyable and to avoid potential problems, plan your routes to avoid stiles and livestock with their young. In many areas, dogs must be kept under close control, often on a lead. Farmers may not be sympathetic if they see your dog chasing their livestock, so control your dog to keep it out of trouble on farmland.

Stiles through and over walls or fences are not always designed with dogs in mind. Having to frequently lift your dog over obstructions is tiring and frustrating. This may be OK if you own a Jack Russell terrier, but not much fun with a Doberman.

TOP T!P

Check maps and reconnoitre routes carefully to ensure they are 'dog-friendly'.

Popularity

Walking is a very popular recreational activity. Here are some figures to illustrate this:

- 9.1 million adults in England, or 22% of the population, walk recreationally for at least 30 minutes in four weeks.
- In Scotland, 30% of adults walk at least 3km/2miles recreationally in four weeks. 31.6% of adults in Wales walk for at least 3km/2miles in four weeks.
- Around 63% of English adults walk for leisure at least once per year, and around 20 million people say they walk for leisure at least once a month.
- Over 2 billion adult days are spent walking as a leisure pastime every year in the UK.
- Walking is the joint most popular activity (along with eating out) for people taking days out in England.
- The number of English adults walking recreationally for at least 30 minutes every month increased by 954,700 (around 10%) between 2006 and 2008.

INFO

Visit the Ramblers Association website at:
www.ramblers.org.uk

Inspiration or Perspiration?

“Enthusiasm is the great hill-climber.”

Elbert Hubbard
US author (1856—1915)

Chapter 2

Inspiration or Perspiration?

Something for everyone

Recreational walking covers a broad range of activities, from gentle ambles to serious mountain expeditions. The great thing about walking is that pretty much everyone can enjoy it. Walking trips can be tailored to match your fitness level and to the amount of time you have available.

How tough?

How strenuous a walk and how long it takes to complete are determined by the following:

- Your fitness level.
- Distance walked.
- Height climbed (and descended).
- Weight carried.
- Terrain.
- Weather conditions.
- Altitude.

Matching these factors to your capabilities is the key to a pleasurable day's walking.

Types of walks

Recreational walking can be broadly categorised as follows:

1. Low walks.
2. High walks.
3. Long distance walks.
4. Hiking and trekking.

1. Low walks

These walks are characterised by flat or undulating terrain – rolling hillsides, country lanes, and woodland. It's the sort of walking where you are rarely out-of-breath, unable to speak to companions and passers-by. These are the sort of walks where flora and fauna are more abundant – perfect for those interested in natural history. For the most part, it is easy-going walking – ideal for novices, the less fit, and those people who prefer inspiration to perspiration.

2. High walks

These walks take in mountain tops and ridges. This is tougher walking, with steeper, more rugged terrain and potentially harsher weather conditions. High level walks have a wild feel. The walking is physically more demanding. Those venturing into mountainous places must be well prepared – with suitable clothing, footwear, and equipment. Fitness and the ability to navigate along mountain paths in remote areas are essential.

The landscape tends to be bleaker and the wildlife is less abundant than at lower levels, but this is compensated by the spectacular views that can be enjoyed.

3. Long distance walks

The UK has many long distance walks, abbreviated as LDWs. These are challenging walks, to be completed in one long push or over several days, or even weeks. Though many are low level – they are long in distance. Classics include the Coast-to Coast Walk, The Pennine Way, and Offa's Dyke Path.

Long distance walkers have to be well organised and plan ahead. Food and accommodation has to be booked and organised. 'Purists' believe that they should be self-sufficient, carrying tents, food and extra clothing in their rucksacks. Others like to 'go light', using hotels or bed and breakfasts along the way, and carrying as little as possible. On some of these routes, companies can be booked to transport your belongings from one stage of the walk to the next.

Long distance walks are hard. Walking day-after-day is not everyone's cup of tea (especially when it is pouring down with rain). Days can be long, and being with the same companions for extended periods can sometimes cause difficulties.

Completing a long distance walk is a good way of exploring new areas and getting to the 'finishing line' is a great achievement – of which to be proud.

INFO

The LDWA is an Association of people with the common interest of walking long distances. Their website contains lots of useful information: **www.ldwa.org.uk**

4. Hiking and trekking

Hiking and trekking are terms that are mainly used for overseas walking activities. Hiking is a term generally used in North America and Canada, whilst trekking is typically used to describe multi-day walks in Asia.

Hiking and trekking are walks that are demanding, often crossing difficult terrain in remote locations. Many routes are at higher altitudes, where acclimatisation and proper equipment is essential.

Getting to far-flung places requires extended periods of travel, sometimes in arduous conditions, and without any home comforts. These trips are for the more adventurous, who have a good level of fitness and mental toughness.

Trekking and hiking holidays are very popular. Many companies offer guided trips in all parts of the world. They are an excellent way to see exciting new places, immerse yourself in different cultures, and meet fascinating people.

Other walking styles

Power walking

Power walking is an activity that aims to improve or sustain your fitness. It is less about rambling through the countryside and more about getting exercise. Power walking is often undertaken through urban areas and parks. Participants wear gym or running clothing and use running shoes as footwear.

Power walking involves walking at speed, often with exaggerated arm movements. The aim is to raise your heart and breathing rate in order to get an aerobic workout. Muscles are exercised too. It is a good way to get, and keep, fit. It is a 'low impact' form of exercise, gentler on your body than jogging or running, but with many of the same fitness benefits.

Nordic walking

Nordic walking is an increasingly popular phenomenon, with enthusiastic participants throughout the world. It is best described as cross-country skiing without the skis. Walking poles are used in order to exercise the arms and upper body, thereby improving the overall workout.

Specially adapted walking/ski poles are used by Nordic walkers. These have uniquely shaped handgrips, which allow the poles to be used at a shallower angle than traditional walking poles. The tips of the Nordic poles hit the ground behind the walker, and provide added traction.

Nordic poles are usually one piece, non-collapsible poles. They come in different lengths, so it's important to get the correct size for your height.

TOP T!P

To calculate the correct Nordic pole size, multiple your height (in centimetres) by 0.68, and then round up or down to the nearest 5cm.

Scrambling

Scrambling may feature in some of your more adventurous outdoor walks. In case you are wondering, it has nothing to do with eggs. Scrambling is where you cross rocky terrain using hands as well as feet. Though not as technically demanding as rock-climbing, routes can be exposed and exhilarating (or dangerous and terrifying, depending on your point of view). Famous mountain scrambles in the UK include Striding Edge in the Lake District, and Crib Goch in Snowdonia, Wales.

Care must be taken when scrambling. Only attempt scrambles that are within your capabilities and be properly equipped. For safety reasons, some scrambles require ropes and other climbing equipment.

Do your research before going scrambling in a new area. There are many scrambling guidebooks available, and information and photographs of scrambling routes can be obtained on the internet. Local outdoor retailers are an excellent source of information and advice, too.

Dangers of scrambling

Be aware that varying weather conditions can dramatically change the nature of a route. A route that is easy to cross in summer sunshine, can be treacherous in ice or snow. Rain and high winds make scrambling much more difficult, too. You should note that scrambling is a potentially dangerous activity and fatal accidents happen even on the lowest graded scrambles.

Scrambling grades

Scrambling routes are graded: the higher the number, the more difficult the scramble. Traditionally, English guidebooks and websites have graded them 1, 2, 3 and 3S (serious), although some are now replacing the '3S' with a '4'. The Scottish system uses 1 to 5. A description of English scrambling grades are below.

- **Grade 1** – rough or exposed walks, with difficult steps where hands and feet are needed. Route finding is usually obvious and escape or retreat is usually possible.
- **Grade 2** – a more serious undertaking. The scrambling is more difficult and continuous. A rope may be required. Route finding and escape or retreat is more difficult.
- **Grade 3** – added exposure, tricky route finding, lack of escape or retreat and increased difficulty, pushes up the grade to '3'. A rope is advisable, even for rock climbers.
- **Grade 3(S)** – used in some guidebooks to denote a particularly serious grade 3 scramble. Though not as technically difficult or sustained as true rock climbs, they can contain individual moves that are as hard as some climbing grades.

TOP T!P

To enjoy your first taste of scrambling, accompany an experienced scrambler or attend a scrambling course.

Gear Freak

“Wisdom oft lurks beneath a tattered coat.”

Caecilius Statius
Roman poet (220 BC—168 BC)

Chapter 3
Gear Freak

These boots are made for walking

Boots are your most important piece of walking equipment. Your day can be ruined by an ill-fitting pair of boots. So beat those blisters and care for those toes – invest in properly fitted boots. Comfort, support and a good sole are your priorities.

If you are looking to buy a new pair of boots – where do you start? There is such a bewildering array in the shops today. Should you buy leather or fabric boots? Two season or three season? Should you buy trail shoes rather than boots?

Buying the right footwear

- Determine what type of walking you will mainly be doing.
- Buy your boots in the afternoon or after you have been on your feet for some time (your feet swell).
- Visit a reputable outdoor retailer and ask their advice.
- Wear the socks you intend to go walking in.
- Try different brands of boots.
- Give the boots an in-shop workout – walk around, jump, hop, and see which feel most comfortable.
- Don't be rushed into a purchase.

- If you have a limited budget – spend it on boots rather than other equipment.

TOP T!P

Women's boots offer an alternative fit for men with smaller, narrower feet.

What's the correct fit?

1. A snug fit without any 'pinch-points'.
2. Good support around your ankles and feet.
3. Your toes shouldn't touch the front of the boot.
4. Your toes shouldn't touch the top of the boot.
5. As you walk, the heel of the boot should move in unison with the heel of your foot.
6. While standing, slide your feet towards the toe of each boot – you should be able to put your index finger down between your heel and the inside of the boot.

Season ratings

1 season – soft, flexible insole, fabric uppers, limited water resistance, suitable for walking on easy paths.

2 season – more robust, flexible sole, aggressive tread pattern, limited ankle support, may have waterproof qualities.

3 season – stiffer sole, greater support, leather or leather/fabric upper, better waterproof qualities.

4 season – stiffened sole, leather upper, crampon compatible, greater insulation and waterproof qualities.

INFO

Trail shoes are a lighter, cooler alternative to boots. But because they do not provide ankle support, and don't keep your feet as dry in wet weather, they are best suited for easy terrain and dry conditions.

A guide to 'boot-speak'

Last – A piece of equipment around which a boot is made.

Cleat – The thick tread which projects from the boot's sole. Toe box – The front of the boot that protects your toes.

Upper – The outer, upper covering of the boot. Can be made from leather, fabric or plastic.

Midsole – The part of the boot sandwiched between the sole and the area under the insole. This provides support, stiffness and stability.

Insoles/footbeds – Part of the boot on which your foot sits. Removable for drying purposes. Tailor made insoles can be purchased for walkers with specific foot conditions.

Crampon connections – Part of the boot onto which crampons can be fitted.

FASCINATING FACT

The foot contains 26 bones, 33 joints, 19 muscles and 107 ligaments.

"When you have worn out your shoes, the strength of the shoe leather has passed into the fibre of your body. I measure your health by the number of shoes and hats and clothes you have worn out."

Ralph Waldo Emerson
American essayist (1803—1882)

Breaking-in your boots

Buying a new pair of boots, then heading out for a long walk, is likely to result in blisters. Boots need time to soften and ease into the shape of your feet. This process is called 'breaking-in' your boots.

Break in your boots by wearing them for short periods. You will feel your boots becoming more comfortable, as the boots 'relax' and your feet get used to them. If you encounter any problems with your boots during this time, seek advice from the shop you bought them from.

Modern boot designs and materials have reduced the time needed to break in a pair of boots. Lightweight fabric boots require only a short period, whilst heavier weight, leather boots benefit from a longer period of breaking in.

Insoles

Some people's feet need extra support. Certain foot conditions can be painful and also lead to knee, hip and back problems, as body posture is thrown off balance by unsupported feet. Custom-made insoles, or orthotics, can help. If you think you may need them, seek advice from a physiotherapist or podiatrist.

For less severe conditions, inexpensive, off-the-shelf versions are available. Many outdoor retailers also sell shock absorbing insoles that help keep your feet comfortable and reduce impact on your joints.

INFO

Flat Feet – correctly termed Pes Planus – is a biomechanical foot problem, where the arch of the foot appears flattened. This can cause an unnatural inward rolling motion of the foot – called 'over pronation'.

Boots and crampon compatibility

Only certain combinations of boot and crampon types are regarded as safe, so please take note.

A grading system is used to classify boots and crampons (see the section on crampons – page 51). The grades explain which combinations of boots and crampons are safe to use. If you are unsure about the grade of your boots, or whether they are safe to use with crampons, seek advice from a reputable outdoor retailer.

Boot grades

B0 – Flexible walking boots. UNSUITABLE for use with any type of crampon, since these boots can be easily bent to an angle of 45 degrees or more.

B1 – Stiff mountain walking boots. The sole of this type of boot can be bent with some effort to an angle of 10 to 45 degrees. Compatible with C1 crampons only (To be used for limited periods or in emergencies).

B2 – Semi-rigid mountaineering boots. These soles can only be bent to an angle of 10 degrees or less with some effort. Compatible with C2 crampons but might also take C1 crampons.

B3 – Fully rigid winter climbing and mountaineering boots. Compatible with C3 crampons but might also take C1 and C2 type crampons.

Clothing for cool, wet conditions

Layers

Dress for the outdoors by adopting the 'onion principle' – plenty of layers. This gives you the flexibility to take layers off to cool down or add layers to warm up. Air is trapped between each layer of clothing, which warm with your body heat and act as added insulation against the elements.

When setting out on your walks, it's usually best to begin by feeling a little cool. You will soon warm up as you walk.

Choosing the correct combination and type of clothing comes with experience. Different climates and weather conditions require different approaches.

Quick dry

Wear garments that dry quickly. Especially if you are walking on consecutive days. There is nothing worse than the cold, clammy feeling of putting on yesterday's damp clothes.

TOP T!P

After walking for 10 minutes, stop and adjust your boots and clothing to ensure that you are comfortable.

Base layers

Wicking

A base layer is your first layer of clothing, which lies next to your skin. It should 'wick away' moisture – which helps keep you dry and warm. Think of 'wicking' as a mini conveyor belt that transports moisture from the surface of your skin, through the base layer, and out the other side. Some fabrics are much better at this than others. Garments labelled as 'high wicking' mean they are high speed 'conveyor belts'. Fabric that doesn't wick properly becomes wet and is less effective at insulating.

Avoid cotton

Cotton garments, including cotton underwear, should be avoided, as they absorb moisture and leave you feeling damp and cold. Instead, buy high wicking underwear, which is much more comfortable. You can also wash and dry these items quickly; perfect for when you are away from home.

Insulating layers

Mid layers are all about insulation: they keep you warm. Examples are fleecy shirts and the traditional fleece pullover or jacket. A good quality fleece offers excellent insulation, and is lightweight but not bulky. Some fleece materials have windblocking qualities; useful if you want to wear them in cold, windy conditions, without an outer layer.

Wear a couple of layers of insulating garments. On cold days, a lightweight fleecy shirt under a heavier fleece jacket works well. You can unzip the jacket to cool down, if necessary, without having to take off a layer of clothing.

Soggy

On a hard day's walk, anything you put into your mid-layer garment pockets can become damp, due to water vapour escaping from your body. Paying for your end-of-walk pint with a soggy ten-pound note is a little embarrassing. Protect susceptible items by placing them in a small plastic bag.

Other useful features

Flexibility

Flexibility is the key to a good layering system. Hoods and elasticated cuffs help you retain heat. Zips and vents allow you to make adjustments without putting on or taking off garments. Pockets enable you to keep important items and snacks close to hand.

Colour

Dark coloured garments are less obtrusive, making you less visible to other walkers and to wildlife. Dark garments don't show the dirt and appear cleaner for longer – especially useful for multi-day trips.

TOP T!P
Add a small piece of tape or elastic cord to small zips to make them easier to manipulate whilst wearing gloves, in cold weather.

Outer layers

Your outer layer is a barrier to the elements. It keeps out the rain and wind. The best garments use fabrics that, cleverly, allow water vapour from your body to escape whilst keeping out the rain. These are known as 'breathable' fabrics. The best breathable fabrics allow water vapour to escape quickly, preventing your clothing from becoming soggy when you are exercising hard. These tend to be expensive, though you can buy less expensive fabrics that do a similar job.

Protection from the rain

Waterproof jackets – useful features:

- An adjustable hood that fits your head properly (and moves with you when you to turn your head).
- A stiffened peak at the front of your hood.
- A pocket big enough to carry a map.
- Underarm zips – allowing you to vent the coat, to cool down.
- Adjustable cuffs and collar.
- Clips to attach gloves and a compass.
- Storm flaps over zips, to keep out the worst weather.

INFO
Climbing and mountaineering jackets tend to be shorter fitting for ease of movement, and to allow harnesses to be fitted.

“Make your feet your friend.”

J. M. Barrie
Scottish novelist & dramatist (1860—1937)

Waterproof trousers

Wearing a waterproof coat and gaitors protects most of your torso and legs from rain, so wearing waterproof trousers is often unnecessary. However, in very wet or cold conditions, they can be useful. Putting on waterproof trousers in the rain is tricky and the insides of your trousers can become dirty from your muddy boots. Before putting on your waterproof trousers, put your foot into a plastic bag, then slip your foot into your trouser leg. Your foot glides in easily and your trousers are kept clean. Waterproof trousers that incorporate side zips and press studs are easier to put on. They can also be vented when you are feeling too warm.

Wearing glasses in the rain

Wearing glasses in the rain is frustrating. If only they came with mini windscreen wipers! A waterproof jacket, with a rigid peak, is a blessing for spectacle wearers walking in the rain. This, worn with a peaked cap pulled well down, is a good combination to keep the rain off your glasses. Alternatively, invest in contact lenses (if suitable for you). This will put an end to your wet and misted-up glasses.

Extra Protection from the cold

Headwear for cold conditions

An estimated 30–50% of your body heat is lost through your head. Wearing a hat on cold days reduces heat loss significantly. If you are feeling cold, the first thing you should do is put on your hat. In cold, windy conditions, headwear made of windblock material performs best.

Glove Love

Your fingers are often the first things to feel the cold, so it is important to wear suitable gloves. Windblock material keeps your hands warm very effectively. In freezing conditions, try a pair of very thin gloves inside a thicker pair of gloves or mittens – this allows you to remove your outer gloves without exposing your skin to the elements. Useful when you need to use your compass or to unwrap a chocolate bar.

To prevent your outer gloves from blowing away in high winds, connect them to your coat sleeves with a small clip or length of elastic. It may remind you of your early school days, but it really works.

Neck warmers and scarves

These days, scarves seem to have been replaced with the ubiquitous Buff™ – a versatile piece of clothing that can be used as a neck warmer, headwear, and sweatband. This is available in light and heavy weight versions. Similar 'neck gaitors' are available from other manufacturers. Worn as a neck warmer, these help to retain body heat and shield your neck from the cold. They also prevent rain from trickling down your neck and soaking your clothes.

TOP T!P

Each time you set off from a rest stop, spend a few seconds checking the ground to make sure that you haven't left anything behind.

Very low temperatures

Insulated jackets

Sometimes, weather conditions require special clothing. In very cold, dry conditions, an insulated jacket is an essential bit of kit. These jackets can easily be packed into a stuff sack.

The best quality ones are filled with goose down, chosen for its excellent insulating qualities. Less expensive jackets contain natural and/or synthetic materials. Although many have a showerproof outer membrane, you should avoid wearing these jackets during rain. If water penetrates the insulating material, its thermal properties are greatly reduced, and they take a very long time to dry out.

Hot, dry conditions

Clothing

Garments should help you keep cool and protect you from the harmful rays of the sun. Light coloured clothing reflects sunlight and also discourages insects. Loose fitting garments with vents are much more versatile than those without. Choose lightweight, quick-dry fabrics.

Headwear for hot conditions

Hats with a wide brim protect your head and face from the sun, keeping you cooler and protecting you from heat-related injuries. Peaked caps keep the sun off your face and, when worn with a neck flap, also protect the back of your neck. Light coloured hats keep your head the coolest. In very hot conditions, soak your hat in clean water before wearing it.

Bandanas are comfortable and lightweight and help keep perspiration out of your eyes. They can be soaked in water easily, to help cool you down. Unlike a wide brimmed hat, they don't shade your face from sun but they do take up much less space in your kit.

Sock it to 'em

Socks keep your feet warm and, when worn properly, are your first line of defence against blisters. Socks come in a variety of thicknesses: thin socks for warm conditions, thick socks for cold conditions. You can also buy very thin sock liners.

When buying socks, keep to the main brands. Try new socks on short walks before wearing them for longer periods. Once you are happy with a particular brand and type of socks, stick with it. Beware of chopping and changing sock thicknesses, as this may result in blisters. You may find that wearing sock liners under a medium thickness pair of socks is the best solution for foot comfort and to avoid blisters.

Rucksacks

The first thing to ask yourself is: What do I intend to use it for? Do you want a rucksack for short, summer walks or do you want to trek to Everest base camp with it?

You can then determine the required capacity, durability and features of your rucksack. The more you need to carry, the bigger your rucksack needs to be; long, adventurous trips require hardwearing materials; the items you carry and how you use them dictate which features are important.

Fitting a rucksack

1. Add some weight to the rucksack – to match the sort of items you will be carrying.
2. Loosen all straps on the rucksack.
3. Fit the hipbelt so that it sits on top of your hips (not around your waist) and tighten.
4. Tighten the shoulder straps.
5. Tighten any load adjusters (located above your shoulders), ensuring your shoulder straps fit snugly.
6. Tighten the chest strap.
7. Walk around the shop, and preferably up steps, to see how it feels.
8. Adjust the back length, if necessary (and if adjustable); repeat steps 1-7.

INFO

Alpine/climbing rucksacks tend to be straight-sided packs, without side pockets or other external features that could become snagged whilst climbing.

Rucksack sizes

The capacity of a rucksack is measured in litres. This is usually stated as a number followed by 'L' (for litre). Your choice depends on how much you intend to carry. Use the following as a guide:

- **Up to 25 litres** – for carrying minimal walking gear.
- **25 to 35 litres** – for a day's winter walking gear.
- **35 to 55L litres** – for serious winter walking, climbing and day mountaineering.
- **55 to 75L litres** – for backpacking, trekking and mountaineering.
- **75L+** – for serious/self-sufficient multi-day expeditions.

Variable volumes

Many rucksacks display two numbers, 55+10 litres for example. This means that the standard capacity of the rucksack is 55 litres but can be expanded by a further 10 litres, by expanding lids, gussets and pockets, etc.

Rucksack features

Try different brands of rucksacks. They are all shaped slightly differently. Some will fit your body shape better than others. Some designs are better suited to women's body shapes, and some are designed specifically for women. Useful features include adjustable frames (to fit different length backs) and easy access pockets, including pockets for water carriers. Choose a comfortable, padded waistband when you are planning to carry heavy loads.

TOP T!P

Tape-up the loose straps on your rucksack. This prevents them from flailing you in high winds.

Rainy days

Most rucksacks are not waterproof, though some now incorporate rain covers. Protect the contents of your rucksack from the rain by enclosing them in a plastic bag – a bin liner is perfect. You can purchase 'dry bags', which do the same job at a higher price. Remember to protect items like wallets and cameras stored in outer pockets, too. Separate rain covers that fit over the outside of your rucksack can be bought from outdoor retailers.

Pole position

Ten years ago, very few people used walking poles. Now their 'tip-tap' can be heard echoing around every mountainside. They seem to be the 'must have' accessory. Poles are useful. They reduce your body weight from impacting on your knees and can be used to aid balance.

Poles vary in price according to the materials used to make them. You will pay a premium for strong, lightweight materials, such as carbon fibre or titanium. Pick poles that suit your hand shape and size, as grips vary widely.

When using poles, put your hands up through the handle hoops before resting them on the grips. For most conditions, set the height of your poles so that your forearms are at 90 degrees to the poles. Shorten your poles when ascending steep ground and lengthen them when descending.

TOP T!P

Cover the spikes of your walking poles with rubber caps to prevent damage to the environment.

Gaitors

Gaitors wrap around your lower legs and are attached to your boots by clips and straps. They can be a little awkward to use at first but you quickly get used to them. Gaitors keep water and snow out of your boots and keep the lower part of your legs warm and dry (You can even paddle across

"The best remedy for a short temper is a long walk."

Jacqueline Schiff
Author

shallow streams in them and avoid filling your boots). They also protect the bottom of your trousers from getting soaked or caked in mud.

Good quality gaitors are expensive but they offer better insulation, breathability, and are more hardwearing.

TOP T!P

Ensure your gaitor straps are securely tucked away to prevent you tripping.

Shine a light

A torch is a useful accessory to have in your rucksack. Head torches are the most convenient, allowing you to keep your hands free for checking your map or using walking poles. Torches can also be used to signal for help. Make sure you have plenty of life in your batteries and take a spare set with you, in case they fail.

Things to consider when buying a head torch:

- Battery life.
- Fit and comfort.
- Stability.
- Weight.
- Ease of use.
- Adjustability of beam.

Your eyes are wonderful things. They can adapt to very low levels of light. If you are navigating at night, rather than rushing to use your torch, give your eyes ten minutes to adjust. Switching on your torch switches off your 'night vision'. If you do need to use your torch to check your map, a red lens allows you to use it whilst limiting the impact on your night vision.

Thirst quenchers

Drinks carriers

There are many kinds of drinks carriers on the market – from sports bottle styles to bag and tube systems that look more at home in a hospital ward.

Bag and tube

It is important to stay hydrated when walking and a drinks carrier that is accessible makes this much easier. The bag and tube systems win hands down on this – delivering drinks without the need to stop, unpack bottles and undo lids. However, they are more expensive than standard drinks bottles and are more difficult to clean.

Bottles

If you prefer more traditional water bottles, choose robust ones made from aluminium or toughened plastic. They are hardwearing and will last many years. A wide necked bottle even allows you to add a tea bag for a cuppa whilst camping.

Your drinks bottles and tubes should be well insulated if you intend to use them in very low temperatures.

TOP T!P

If you are planning to walk in hot conditions, fill your drinks bottles and put them in your freezer the night before you go walking. You will have refreshingly cold drinks for your walk. Don't fill your bottles to the top, as the water will expand as it freezes.

Flasks

If you want to take a hot drink with you, use an 'unbreakable flask'. Standard flasks are easily smashed in the outdoors.

Specialist equipment for winter

Crampons are those spiky little things that you strap to the bottom of your boots to prevent you from slipping on ice or hard snow. They can also be used for ice climbing.

Boot compatibility

It is important to ensure that your boots are 'crampon compatible'. In other words, that your boots are safe to have crampons fitted to them. There are different styles of crampons, which can only be used with particular boot types. Incorrectly fitted crampons can be lethal – so seek advice when buying a pair. (See *Boots and crampon compatibility* on page 36.)

Walking in crampons

Walking in crampons does take a bit of practice, in order to avoid ripping your trouser bottoms or stabbing your ankles.

Crampon grades:

C1 – Articulated or flexible walking crampons attached with simple straps. These crampons mostly have ten points, two at the front and eight at the back. This type is light and simple, and is best for occasional use.

C2 – Articulated or flexible step-in crampons attached with a heel clip and a toe strap. These commonly have twelve points, giving the best combination of ease of attachment, walking comfort, and climbing performance. A good choice for general mountaineering and lower grade climbs.

C3 – Stiff or fully rigid crampons attached with a heel clip and toe bail. This type is normally equipped with twelve or more points, and often with adjustable front points. They are the best choice for pure climbing.

Properly fitted

The plan and profile of your crampons should match the sole of your boots. Crampons must be correctly matched and securely fitted to your boots to ensure that they are safe to use. Ensure that they are correctly adjusted and know how to fit them before using them.

TOP T!P

Wear gaitors to protect your lower legs and trouser bottoms from crampons.

Snow shoes

Wading through knee-high snow is no joke. It is time-consuming and exhausting. Travelling in these conditions is much easier when using snow shoes. These tennis racket-like pieces of kit spread your body weight over a wide surface area, enabling you to walk on the surface of snow without sinking. Though they are not seen in the UK very often, they are popular in snowy regions of the world.

Cool as an ice axe

You have to admit it, heading into the UK mountains with your ice axe makes you look pretty cool – except if it is the middle of summer, then you just look plain silly. An ice axe gives you a certain swagger. You are not just any old walker – you are now a mountaineer. Expect nods of approval and admiring glances from those around you. But aside from looking the part, an ice axe is used for:

- Cutting steps.
- As a means to climb steep snow and ice.
- Arresting a fall.
- Using as a belay point (anchor).
- For added stability when walking.

TOP T!P

Attend a winter skills course to learn how to use an ice axe properly.

Types of axe

Ice axes with straight shafts (50–55cm) and gently curving picks are suitable for winter walking and non-technical mountain ascents, whilst curved axes with reverse picks are used for technical climbing.

There are two types of CE mark (European standards) for axes:

- **B-rated ('Basic')** axes are intended for hill walking, and have shafts strong enough to use them as belay. Other tests check the strength of the pick and security of the head.
- **T-rated ('Technical')** tools are intended for climbing and mountaineering. They are at least 30–40% stronger than B-rated axes, to allow for more extreme use.

FASCINATING FACT

The toothed, pointed end of an ice-axe head is called the 'pick' and the flat, wide end of the head is known as the 'adze'.

Nutrition for Walkers

"Never eat more than you can lift."

Miss Piggy
Muppet

Chapter 4

Nutrition for Walkers

Healthy eating

Healthy eating is the foundation of a healthy lifestyle. Appropriate calorie intake and a properly balanced diet provides you with the energy needed to complete your walks, and the nutrients to recover afterwards. Eating healthily helps keep you strutting your stuff, whilst poor nutrition contributes to illness, injury and lethargy. Healthy food is the best walking fuel.

Healthy eating doesn't mean you have to give up all the things you enjoy. You do not have to starve yourself either. It is about eating and drinking more of the things that are beneficial to your body, and eating less of the food types that are not so good for you.

A balanced diet

To stay healthy, we need to eat a balanced diet of foods containing all the nutrient groups – protein, carbohydrates, fat, vitamins and minerals. A balanced diet is one where these foods are eaten in the right proportions:

- Carbohydrates = 50% of total calorie intake
- Protein = 20%
- Fats = 30% *

*with less than 10% coming from saturated fat.

Regular sports participants benefit from a far greater carbohydrate intake.

Diet for regular sports participants

- Carbohydrates = 60%
- Protein = 15%
- Fats = 25%

Food groups

- **Protein** – required for tissue growth and repair. Protein rich foods include meat, fish, eggs, milk, dairy foods, nuts, beans, and lentils.
- **Carbohydrates** – are used by the body to provide energy. There are two important types: simple and complex carbohydrates. Simple (or 'sugary') carbohydrates are found in sugary foods, sweets and fruit. Complex (or 'starchy') carbohydrates are found in pasta, bread, potatoes, cereals, and rice. Simple carbohydrates give you a quick boost to your blood sugar levels, which soon slumps. Complex carbohydrates typically release energy more gradually, over a longer period of time.
- **Fats** – are used as a source of energy, to help absorb some vitamins, and contain some essential fatty acids. Saturated fats are found in meat pies, sausages, pastry, cakes, and cream. Unsaturated fats are found in oily fish, nuts and seeds, avocados, olive oil spreads and vegetable oils. Nutritionists recommend that we cut down on our intake of saturated fats and have unsaturated instead.

FASCINATING FACT

Carbohydrates and proteins contain 4 calories per gram and fats contain 9 calories per gram.

More about carbohydrates

Carbohydrate is stored in the liver and muscles as glycogen. These stores are relatively small and are depleted by exercise. When you run out of glycogen – you run out of energy. Your reserves need to be topped up by a new intake of carbohydrates.

Carbo-loading

If you are planning a long, strenuous walk – load up on carbohydrates the night before and prior to heading out. Also, make sure you take carbohydrate-rich food and snacks with you.

Replenishing

The first two hours after exercising is the best time to replenish your glycogen stores. After this period, glycogen replacement slows down. Load up on carbohydrates soon after a hard walk, to refuel your muscles and speed-up recovery. Aim to eat 1 gram of carbohydrate per kilogram of your body weight within two hours of finishing a hard walk, then repeat this amount two hours later.

TOP T!P

Always carry some high energy emergency rations with you. You never know when you will need them.

Calories burned

The amount of calories you burn whilst walking depends on several factors:

- Your age, body composition and weight.
- Your fitness level.
- The intensity – how tough a walk.
- The duration of your walk.

Calorie consumption

For example, the estimated calorie expenditure for a healthy young man weighing 70 kg (11 stone) is as follows:

- Walking on flat ground at a speed of 4 kilometres per hour (approx. 2.5 miles per hour) will use 220 calories per hour.
- Travelling uphill with a 7 kg (approx.15.5lb) rucksack will use 580 calories per hour.

Calorie consumption increases substantially if you carry a heavy rucksack, climb steep terrain, walk into a strong wind, or cross deep snow. Cold conditions also cause your body to burn calories at a greater rate, to maintain your core temperature. Your calorie intake should take this into account.

Heart-rate monitors

You can get an accurate assessment of your calorie consumption whilst walking by using a heart-rate monitor. Yes, another gadget, but they can be very useful.

Heart–rate monitors look like a watch; in fact, some are incorporated into standard watches and altimeters. They work by listening to your heart rate, usually via a comfortable strap that fits around your chest. This transmits information to the unit on your wrist, which is used to count the calories you burn during exercise.

You start the 'count' as you commence your walk and stop it once you've finished. The monitor displays the total number of calories you have burned. Other data, such as maximum heart-rate reached, suggested exercise intensity, and training goals can also be accessed.

If you are technologically minded, some units let you download this information to your computer for further analysis and as a permanent training record.

Losing fat

It is disconcerting to realise that a pound of fat contains 3500 calories. In other words, to lose a pound of the wobbly stuff, you have to burn an extra 3500 calories.

Experts tell us that the optimal fat-burning walking speed is a pace at which we breathe heavily, but are still able to carry on a conversation. At this pace, your heart rate will normally be working at around 60–70% of its maximum rate.

INFO

Losing fat is best achieved by a combination of eating less and exercising more.

Maximum heart rate

Your maximum heart rate can be estimated by subtracting your age from 220*. For example: for a person aged 40 – maximum heart rate is 220 minus 40 equals 180 beats per minute. So, training at 60% of maximum heart rate means a heart rate of 108 beats per minute.

*This is a quick way of estimating your maximum heart rate and should only be used as a guide.

Dehydration

It is easy to become dehydrated whilst exercising, especially when your focus is on things other than your liquid intake. By the time you feel thirsty, you are already becoming dehydrated.

Impact on performance

Dehydration, even at early stages, can have a detrimental effect on your physical and mental performance. Fluid losses of 5% of body weight can reduce exercise performance by up to 30%. In severe cases, dehydration is fatal. Make sure you are well hydrated before you start walking. Take plenty of liquid refreshment with you – and drink it regularly.

Fluid loss

Even an inactive adult loses almost three and a half litres of water each day: one and a half litres in urine, one litre through breathing, and half a litre through sweating. During exercise, the body's requirement for water is greatly increased. To stave off dehydration when walking, aim to drink 150–200 ml of water every 15 minutes.

“A vigorous five-mile walk will do more good for an unhappy but otherwise healthy adult than all the medicine and psychology in the world.”

Paul Dudley White
Cardiologist (1886—1973)

In hot conditions and during high levels of exertion, the body may not be able to absorb water fast enough to keep pace with its water loss. In these circumstances, it is very important to drink plenty of water before and afterwards, to top up your tank.

Don't be shy

Some people, feeling self-conscious about 'answering the call of nature' in the outdoors, drink minimal amounts of fluid before and during a walk. This isn't good for you, and can be dangerous. Keep well hydrated – there is always a strategically placed boulder or bush to hide behind, to protect your modesty.

TOP T!P

Ensure that your drinks are easily accessible – this encourages you to drink more.

Signs and symptoms of dehydration

Early signs: weakness; tiredness; nausea; dizziness; headache; irritability; low urine output and what is produced is dark coloured and strong smelling.

Later signs: dry mouth and tongue; clumsiness; rapid, weak pulse; pale, inelastic, dry skin; drowsiness.

TOP T!P

When trekking, never pass by a source of good, clean water without filling your water bottles.

Liquid lifesaver

There are situations where you should dramatically increase your intake of liquid:

- High temperatures.
- Humid environments.
- High levels of exertion.
- Altitude.

In these conditions, the body loses water even more quickly through increased perspiration and water vapour loss, due to heavier, more frequent breathing.

High altitude

In hot conditions, and when you are exercising hard, the urge to drink is strong. It can be a different matter when trekking in cold conditions at higher altitudes. Many experienced mountaineers agree that drinking large quantities of liquid greatly improves the body's ability to acclimatise. Drinking can seem more of a chore when temperatures are low. Even so, the key is to drink plenty (5 or 6 litres is typical) before, during and after your day's trek.

Remember to plan for your increased demand for liquid. Carry extra water with you and/or ensure you are able to find drink sources on route.

Purifying water

Why?

Sometimes it is necessary to obtain water from natural sources. When doing so, to prevent water-borne illnesses, it is essential to treat the water before drinking it. Use only clear looking, flowing water, and check upstream for dead animals or other possible pollutants.

How?

Purify water in one of three ways: boiling, disinfection or micro-filtration. Here are the pros and cons of each method:

Boiling water for 2 minutes – kills by high temperature.

- Simple method.
- Certain.
- Requires stoves/pan.
- Costly on fuel.
- Water must be boiled for longer periods at higher altitude.

Disinfection using iodine or chlorine – kills by the actions of chemical agents.

- No additional gear required.
- Low weight/bulk.
- Takes time to work (up to 30 minutes for iodine in very cold water).
- Taste (but Vitamin C powder can be added after water has been purified to improve the taste).
- Not effective at killing Cryptosporidium.
- Iodine – not suitable for pregnant women, children, or those with thyroid problems.

Micro-filtration using a filter – filters particles and pathogens.

- Simple method.
- Requires expensive filter.
- Bulky/heavy.
- Does not guarantee complete removal of viruses (but where these are a problem – get a filter with an iodine element).

- Filter can be damaged by impact and frost.
- Pores may become enlarged and less effective.

Demon drink

Whilst there are few things better than relaxing at a country pub during a good walk, care needs to be taken when mixing alcohol with walking in the countryside. Alcohol can impair your decision-making abilities and affect your ability to navigate. Balance can also be impaired, leading to increased risk of injury from trips and falls.

Alcohol also dehydrates you. So you must take extra care rehydrating your body after consuming your favourite tipple.

Although it is fun to 'let your hair down' when you are away on a walking trip, it's best to be aware of the implications.

Planning Your Walk

“Whoever wants to reach a distant goal must take small steps.”

Saul Bellow
Nobel Prize winning writer (1915—2005)

Chapter 5

Planning Your Walk

I've got a plan!

What do you want to get out of your day's walk? What's your goal? Have you psyched yourself up for something big – a heroic leg-trembling mountain yomp, or do you want to wander around your local forest with your binoculars and your bird watching book?

Are you heading out alone or are there others to consider? If you are planning an outing with friends, are they super fit SAS types or are they overweight with dodgy knees? Planning your walk needs to take this sort of thing into consideration. We look at these and other factors in this chapter.

Using guidebooks

Guidebooks are available for just about every part of the world. They give a flavour of the area – this can include its history, wildlife, and other points of interest. Walks are described and maps show suggested routes. Photographs or drawings are used too. For example, Wainwright's famous guides to the Lake District are brilliant works of art, with hand-drawn maps and beautiful illustrations.

- Take a map with you, too – don't rely solely on your guide book. It's good to have a way of double-checking things.
- Be aware that your guide book may be out of date – there may have been changes to rights of way since publication.
- Treat suggested walk times with caution – your walking speed may vary considerably from that of the author.

- Protect your guide book from the weather by placing it inside a sealable plastic bag.

Planning your route using a map

Whilst some people like to keep their maps in pristine condition, they are simply a tool to be used to aid navigation and plan routes. Draw on your maps if this makes the task of navigating easier. Mark routes with a highlighter pen, making them easier to follow and also to act as a record of the route.

UK Ordnance Survey maps are probably the most accurate maps in the world – carefully surveyed by satellite and, in many cases, double checked by teams of people on the ground. Overseas maps may not be as accurate, and different scales and symbols are used, making them more tricky to follow.

Picking your route

Use a highlighter pen to identify the start and finish points of your intended walk. Pick out points of interests and targets you wish to achieve in the same way. Choose large features you can easily identify during your walk. You can mentally 'tick these off' as you progress along your route.

Use linear features as 'handrails', which you can follow easily, without any complicated navigating. Work out the best route between these points. Highlight the whole route with your highlighter pen, in a colour that makes it easy for your eye to follow once you are outdoors.

Measuring the distance

Use a length of string to measure the route's distance by laying it over your mapped-out path, then measure it against the distance scale at the foot of your map. Or, if you want another gadget, you can use a map measurer – a device with a wheel, which displays your route distance as you roll it over your map.

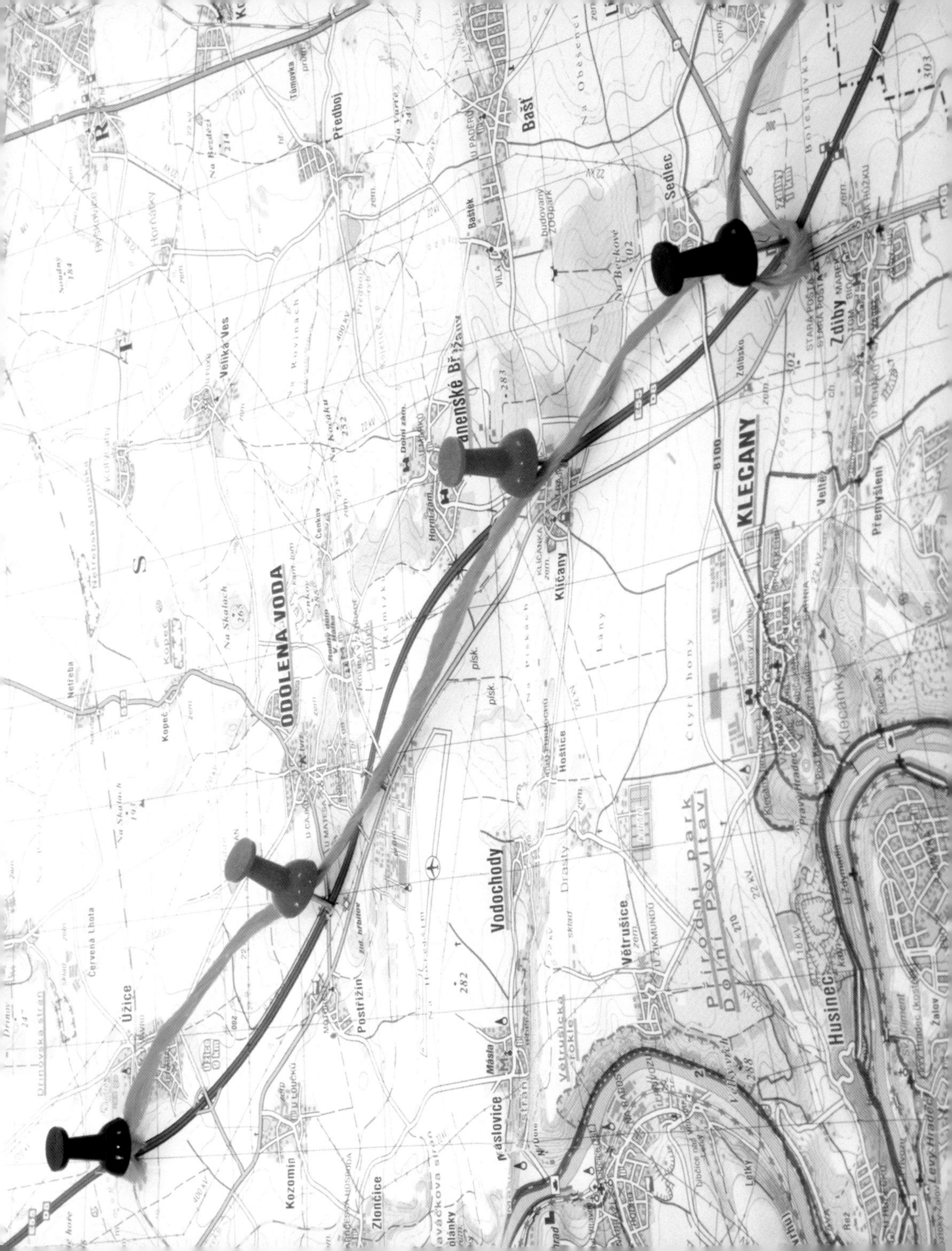

Užice
Kozomín
Zlončice
Postřižín
Máslovice
Vodochody
Větrušice
Odolena Voda
Velká Ves
Předboj
Baště
Sedlec
Klíčany
Hoštice
Klecany
Zdiby
Přemyšlení
Husinec
Veltěž
Přírodní park
Dolní Povltaví

How much climbing?

Next, calculate how many metres of ascent you will be making by counting the contours. For hillwalking, you can make a quick assessment by looking at the altitude of the highest point of your route, and subtracting this from your starting altitude.

For a more accurate result, you must take into account any major undulations along your route. For example, a path along a ridge may ascend and descend several times along its course. Add up the total amount of ascent for all sections of your route – giving you a more accurate picture of how much climbing will be required.

TOP T!P

Plan to do most of your climbing at the start of your walk, when your legs are least tired.

Get suggestions on the internet

Many websites provide you with suggested walking routes, with detailed walk descriptions and even downloadable maps, directions, and G.P.S. co-ordinates.

A fee is often payable, though some sites provide this information free. Type 'downloadable walking routes' or 'free walking guides' into a search engine, such as Google, to find these sites.

Google your walking area

If you are considering walking in a particular area and you want more information about it – search Google. This is a good way of discovering lots of useful information about the area, including photographs and reports from people who have walked there.

TOP T!P

Contact tourist information offices for free walking guides and route suggestions.

Get off my land!

- Double check the course of your intended route, to make sure you have a right of way or a right to roam over the land.
- Always abide by any public safety notices along your route.
- Respect temporary footpath diversions.
- Be aware of local access restrictions, such as during grouse shooting or deer stalking seasons.
- If you discover that a right-of-way has been blocked, report this to the local highways authority.

Route planners

There are three good reasons to use a route planner – before, during and after your walk:

1. **Before:** Helps to plan your route and understand how long your route will take you.
2. **During:** Use it to guide you on your walk.
3. **After:** As a safety back-up if things go wrong.

(A blank route plan is shown on page 182)

Complete a route plan before you start your walk. Split your route down into 'legs' to simplify the planning process. Calculate the overall distance and total height gain and loss. This enables you to estimate how demanding and how long the route will take to complete.

What to include

A route plan should include the following:

- Start location and estimated start time.
- Numbers of people in group.
- Contact numbers (including any accommodation).
- Description of route and grid references.
- Important navigation details, e.g. compass bearings, etc.
- Distance and height gain/loss.
- Anticipated weather conditions.
- End location and estimated finish time.

Leave a copy

Prior to setting out on your route, let a trusted person have a copy of your route plan (photocopy or email), together with your estimated time of return. Arrange to contact them when you are safely back. Leave clear instructions with them as to what to do if you do not make contact.

Use your computer

Modern mapping software makes the job of completing a route plan easy. Routes are highlighted by clicking on the map with your computer's mouse. Route plans, with automatically calculated distances, timings, bearings, and terrain profiles, can be printed off and emailed.

Factors to consider

How much time?

Use the walking time guide discussed later in this book to estimate the duration of your walk. Use this as a base, but, for greater accuracy, work out your own walking speed, and that of other members of your group. Don't forget to add time for regular rest stops.

Plan for the least fit

Plan your walk with the least fit person in mind. Will they be able to complete the route? How will they affect the overall pace of the walk? Will everyone enjoy the outing, or will different walking speeds and levels of fitness be a cause of frustration amongst your group? Remember, walking is meant to be fun.

Choosing your walking companions

Walking tends to be a more pleasant experience when your companions are like-minded people.

If people have different goals and expectations, problems can arise. Beforehand, make sure everyone knows the type of walk you have in mind, and check that they are happy to come along. Inform inexperienced walkers what to expect and what clothing and equipment they will need.

For challenging walks, such as long-distance routes and multi-day mountain trips, even the best friendships can be tested. Tiredness, stress, and being together for long periods, can put relationships under pressure. Discuss potential problems beforehand and work out ways to have your own space. Aim to maintain an easy going attitude and sense of humour.

Early bath?

What if one of your party is unable or unwilling to go on? Do you have a plan for this? Preparing for this, and having everyone's agreement on the course of action you will take, makes the situation more manageable.

The impact of weather

Weather conditions affect the character of a walk. A route that is an easy summer stroll can be an arduous undertaking in harsh weather conditions.

INFO

The Sport Scotland Avalanche Information Service is an important source of information about snow conditions on Scottish mountains. See: **www.sais.gov.uk**

Heavy rain can swell previously shallow streams into uncrossable torrents; low cloud and mist makes route finding difficult and hinders progress. Strong winds slow walkers down, sometimes literally to a crawl. Choose routes carefully, with these factors in mind.

Plan B

If conditions have deteriorated significantly when you arrive at the start of your intended route, don't be afraid to adjust your plans to make your trip less ambitious and better suited to the conditions. This may mean shortening your route or keeping off high ground. If you do change your plans, remember to inform your trusted person of your new route and estimated return time.

Obtain a weather report

It is important to be aware of weather conditions in the area in which you are intending to walk. For high level walking, where the impact of the weather is often most powerful, an up-to-date weather report is absolutely essential.

Where can you get weather information?

- Websites such as:
  www.metoffice.gov.uk/loutdoor/mountainsafety
  www.metcheck.com
- Webcams can give an insight into weather conditions for particular areas. Search Google for webcams in the area you are planning to walk.

- Tourist Information Centres, and outdoor retailers in popular walking areas, often display weather forecasts for the following few days in their windows.

Hours of daylight

If you are planning a long day's walk, check sunrise and sunset times to make sure you will have enough daylight to complete your route safely. Here is a useful website to get sunrise and sunset times:
www.timeanddate.com/worldclock/sunrise.html

On the website, you can enter the location closest to the area in which you intend to walk, and sunrise and sunset times are automatically displayed *(See page 185)*.

Gear checklist

Make sure you are suitably equipped. The day before your walk, double check that you have everything and that your equipment works properly. This gives you time to make repairs or replace items, if necessary.

Food and drink

Take sufficient food and drink with you, or plan your route to call at a café or pub for refreshments. Some places vary their opening times according to the season. It is worth checking beforehand, to avoid the disappointment of finding your eagerly anticipated watering hole closed.

Checklist

- Boots.
- Socks.
- Waterproof trousers.
- Waterproof jacket.
- Trousers.
- Shirts.
- Fleece jacket.
- Gloves (inners and outers).
- Hat.
- Gaitors.
- Neck warmer/scarf.
- Map and compass (GPS).
- Route planner.
- Torch.
- Food/drink/snacks.
- Rucksack.

Spares 'n' stuff

Remember the following:

- Spare batteries – for your torch and GPS (if you have one).
- Mobile phone – fully charged.
- Cash, including change for car parking.
- Safety whistle.
- First aid kit.
- Blister kit.
- Suncream and sunglasses (for when the sun shines!).
- Lip moisturiser.
- Emergency rations/sweets.
- Emergency shelter/bivvy bag.
- Knife.
- Duct tape – it can be used to repair almost anything.
- Notebook.
- Guidebook.
- Camera – with fully charged battery.

SPIŠSKÁ MAGURA
Ždiar
Mesto Vysoké Tatry
TATRANSKÁ KOTLINA
Lendak

Understanding Maps

“I have an existential map. It has ‘You are here’ written all over it.”

Steven Wright
US comedian and actor (1955—)

Chapter 6

Understanding Maps

Learn to read a map

Getting lost and being forced to ask total strangers which way to go is very embarrassing. It's not good for your 'street cred'. Especially when you are dressed in your colour coordinated, big-label, outdoor outfit. It doesn't do much for your relationships either, particularly if your walking partner isn't seeing the funny side of walking in circles.

But it's not just embarrassing or awkward, there is a serious reason to learn to navigate – getting lost can be life threatening. Each year, people die after losing their way and falling off something steep, or from succumbing to the cold. Learning to navigate properly is simply good sense. Learning to navigate is fun, and being able to find your way confidently adds to your enjoyment of the outdoors.

Maps

Most of us are accustomed to using road maps. Well, maps used for walking are just a bigger scale with more details shown on them. Using a map is not as difficult as you might imagine. They are fascinating things to study. It's surprising what you can discover in your own neighbourhood by studying a map. If you are new to map reading, practise using a map in areas you are familiar with; it's the best way to build confidence.

Map scale

A map is a scaled-down picture of the landscape as seen from above. UK maps suitable for walking typically have a scale of 1:25,000 or 1:50,000.

This means that one unit of measurement on the map equals 25,000 or 50,000 units of distance on the land. In simple terms, this means:

1:25,000 scale

- 1 cm on the map equals 250 metres (25,000 cm) distance on the land.
- 4 cm measured on the map equals 1 kilometre of distance on the land.

1:50,000 scale

- 1 cm on the map equals 500 metres (50,000 cm) distance on the land.
- 2 cm measured on the map equals 1 kilometre.

Pros and cons

Much more detail is displayed on a 1:25,000 map, so this tends to be the most popular scale used by walkers. But before you rush out to buy your 1:25,000 map, 1:50,000 maps have their advantages, too. They tend to show the overall contours of the land more effectively and one map covers a wide geographical area. Also, 1:25,000 maps are not always available for all locations.

Metric and Imperial

Maps use metric units. Stick to using metres and kilometres. It makes map reading and navigation much easier. Maps also display conversion scales, which show both metres/kilometres and feet/miles.

For those who like to use both metric and imperial units, here is a comparison:

- 1.6 km = 1.0 mile
- 5 km = 3.1 miles
- 10 km = 6.2 miles

- 100 metres = 328 feet
- 300 metres = 984 feet
- 600 metres = 1968 feet
- 900 metres = 2952 feet

Map symbols

Maps use symbols to indicate the position of places of interest. These are described in the legend at the edge of the map. It is important to become familiar with most of these. It is essential to be able to recognise footpaths and other rights of way.

Some symbols look alike and can be confused with each other, especially in a howling gale. People have followed symbols for county boundary lines and overhead power lines, thinking they were following footpaths! Double check your symbols before following your route.

Access for walkers

Most land in Britain is privately owned. Walkers have access to certain areas through legislation and access agreements. An up-to-date map is an important tool to ensure that you stay on the 'right side of the law'. In many areas, this means keeping to the right-of-way identified on your map. Other areas allow the walker a 'right to roam'. This is discussed in more detail below.

Rights of way

England and Wales

A 'right-of-way' is the legal right to cross land along a specified route. There are several kinds of rights-of-way.

- **Public footpaths** – open only to walkers. Typically waymarked with yellow arrows.

- **Public bridleways** – open to walkers, cyclists and horse-riders. Often waymarked with blue arrows.
- **Restricted byeways** – open to all non-motorised vehicles. Waymarked with plum-coloured arrows.
- **Byeways open to all traffic** – including motorists.

Rights-of-way are shown as green dashed lines on a 1:25,000 scale map and red dashed lines on a 1:50,000 map. Rights-of-way are not shown on maps of Scotland. *(See the Reference section on page 181 for Rights of Way and Access Symbols for 1:25,000 OS maps).*

Permissive paths

These are not rights-of-way, but are paths that are open to the public, through special permission given by the landowner. This permission can be withdrawn and some paths are closed at certain times of the year.

INFO

Permissive paths and bridleways are normally shown as a series of orange dashed lines on 1:25,000 scale maps.

National trails and long-distance routes

These can be identified by:

- A series of green diamonds – 1:25,000 maps.
- A series of red diamonds – 1:50,000 maps.

Many of these routes have a logo displayed at their start and on waymarkers along their route. An acorn symbol is used in England and Wales and a thistle symbol in Scotland.

Right to roam

England and Wales

Recent legislation has opened-up specific areas of land, classified as: mountain, moor, heath, down and registered common land. The newly opened areas are known as 'access land'. These areas are shown on maps coloured light yellow, surrounded by a pale orange border.

In these areas, the walker can roam freely, without necessarily keeping to particular paths. Restrictions do apply. For example, camping is not allowed and dogs must be kept under close control. Areas may also be closed at certain times of the year.

"My grandmother started walking five miles a day when she was sixty. She's ninety-three today and we don't know where the hell she is."

Ellen DeGeneres
Stand-up comedienne (1958—)

Scotland

Historically, the public has had a right to access all land, unless there was a particular reason to exclude them. The Land Reform Act 2003 confirmed this. There are some exceptions, which are excluded by law, such as railway land, quarries, airfields, and military areas.

Grouse and deer

Certain areas should be avoided during the grouse shooting and deer stalking seasons, for safety reasons. Seek advice from local authorities, tourist information centres, or by visiting **www.snh.org.uk/hillphones**. This website offers an answer-phone message service that provides information on the best routes to use, to avoid disturbing stalking activities in Scotland.

Other rights to roam

Other land on which you have the freedom to roam:

- National Park access land.
- National Trust land.
- Forest Commission woodland.

These areas are identified by the relevant symbols on your map.

TOP T!P

Routes through woodland are sometimes blocked or diverted for safety reasons during forestry operations. Look out for any notices displayed at entry points.

Grid references

On O.S. Maps, Great Britain is covered by 100 kilometre grid squares. Each grid square is identified by two letters, e.g. 'NY'. Each of these

100 kilometre grid squares is further divided into one kilometre square sections – shown as blue lines (grid lines) on your map. We use these to calculate grid references, which enable us to pinpoint positions.

Grid lines

- Grid lines that run from the top to the bottom of the map are known as 'Eastings'.
- Grid lines that run from left to right are known as 'Northings'.

Four-figure grid references

A four-figure grid reference gives the co-ordinates of an area one kilometre square. The four-figure grid reference is made up of two two-digit numbers. The first two digits are taken from the number of the grid line at the bottom of the map (which lines up with the left-hand edge of the kilometre square), the second pair are from the grid line at the side of the map (which lines up with the bottom edge of the kilometre square). Your four-figure grid reference should look something like this: NY 20 14.

TOP T!P

Remember the order in which to read off your digits by using the phrase 'Go into the house and along the corridor before going upstairs' (i.e. read off the digits at the bottom of the map before the digits on the side).

Six-figure grid references

In order to obtain a more precise 'fix' of our position, we must use a six-figure grid reference. This gives the co-ordinates of an area one hundred metres square.

To do this, we need to sub-divide each kilometre box into 100 metre boxes. Maps do not show these lines – it would obscure the rest of the details on the map. Instead, we use a 'Romer Scale' for this. These are displayed on most good compasses, and can be bought separately from outdoor retailers.

A Romer Scale divides up the kilometre squares on your map into 100-metre sections. Its transparent background enables you to place it over your map to pinpoint your position.

To get your six-figure grid reference:

- Place the Romer Scale over your map – line up its corner with the position you wish to pinpoint.
- On your Romer Scale, read off the number that sub-divides the bottom edge of the kilometre square.
- Add this number to the end of your first two-digit number (as obtained in the four-figure reference example).

You now have the first half of your six-figure grid reference.

- On your Romer Scale, now read off the number that sub-divides the edge of the kilometre square.
- Add this number to the end of your second two-digit number.

You now have the second half of your six-figure grid reference. Your grid reference should look something like this: NY 206 145.

TOP T!P

There are separate Romer Scales for 1:25,000 and 1:50,000 maps – use the correct one.

The three 'Norths'

There are three 'Norths' used in navigation and map reading.

- **True North** – the geographical location of the North Pole.

- **Grid North** – the direction in which your map's (eastings) grid lines lead, when following them towards the top of your map.
- **Magnetic North** – the direction in which your compass needle points.

Confused? Then let me explain...

True North

True North is the easiest to understand. It is the physical place at the top of the world and, unless you are a polar explorer, is of very little interest to us as navigators. We use Grid and Magnetic North most often, and need to understand them to navigate properly.

Grid North

Map makers cover their maps in grids, which help us to identify positions more accurately. It also provides a framework from which we can take bearings. This is explained below.

Grid bearings

Eastings are grid lines that run from the top to the bottom of your map. If you slide your finger towards the top of your map, along one of these lines, you are moving on a 'grid bearing' towards Grid North. Slide your finger, towards the bottom of the map, using the same line – you are moving on a 'grid bearing' towards Grid South.

Magnetic North

The earth's magnetic attraction pulls your compass needle round to point to 'Magnetic North'. Very handy. We can use it to find our way. But, you may be thinking, why isn't Grid North the same as Magnetic North? The answer is that the earth's magnetic field is not fixed – it is slowly moving.

The map grid lines are fixed, but we have to account for our compass pointing in a slightly different direction – towards Magnetic North. So we are left having to use the two terms: Grid North and Magnetic North. The difference, in degrees, between Magnetic North and Grid North is displayed on maps. (There is more information about magnetic variation in the next chapter, *Navigating*.)

TOP T!P

Use maps that are up-to-date. This ensures that you make the correct adjustments for magnetic variation.

Contour lines

Contour lines are the fine, brown-coloured lines that appear on your map. They help illustrate the shape of the landscape. A quick glance at your map's contour lines helps identify steep ground. They are shown more densely packed for steep ground, and are more widely spaced for less steep terrain.

Contour lines link points of equal height above sea level. On a 1:25,000 scale map, contour lines are shown at 10-metre intervals in mountainous areas, and 5-metre intervals in lowland areas.

Contour lines are numbered. The numbers show the height of the ground above sea level in metres. For example: a line labelled '150' shows that the ground is 150 metres above sea level at that point.

Every fifth contour line is known as an index contour and is displayed on a map as a thick line.

FASCINATING FACT

The top of the number displayed on a contour line always 'points' uphill.

Estimating steepness

You can estimate the steepness of a slope by counting the number of thick contour lines in 1 cm of the map. Use your compass to measure the distance. Lay the edge of your compass down the slope shown on your map. Its edge should be at 90 degrees to the contour lines. Now, count the number of thick contour lines shown in 1 cm of map. Use the table to estimate its steepness. For example, on a 1:25,000 map, 4 thick contour lines in 1 cm of map indicates a slope with an angle of 40 degrees.

1:25,000 map	Angle of slope	1:50,000 map
1	10 degrees	2
1.8	20 degrees	3.5
3	30 degrees	6
4	40 degrees	8
6	50 degrees	12
8	60 degrees	16

40
60
80
E
100
120
SE
140
160
S
180
200
220

Navigating

“If we don’t change direction soon, we’ll end up where we’re going.”

Irwin Corey
US comedian and actor (1914—)

Chapter 7

Navigating

Orientating your map

Orientate your map so you can more easily pick out and 'tick off' features as you walk along your route. Aligning your map with features in the landscape is also known as 'setting your map'. You can do this in one of two ways:

1. **By sight:** By looking at the terrain and rotating your map so that it orientates with features you can see, such as rivers, footpaths, buildings, etc.

2. **By compass:** (See next section for more details on using your compass.) Rotate the housing on your compass, until the 'N' is lined up with the direction of travel arrow. Lay your compass on your map, with its edge along one of the map's grid lines (Eastings), ensuring that the 'N' on your compass is pointing towards the TOP of your map. You will see the compass needle merrily pointing towards Magnetic North. With the compass on the map, rotate your body until the needle lines up with the 'N' on your compass housing.

Why use a compass?

You may be thinking: Why bother orientating your map using a compass? It's more complicated than doing it by sight. You are right, but sometimes you cannot see any features – in mist, at night, or on featureless terrain. Using a compass to 'set your map' may be the only way.

TOP T!P

To keep your map dry and accessible – use a waterproof map case.

Mapping software

Maps for many popular walking areas are now available as computer software. Some enable you to:

1. Zoom-in on particular features.
2. See a 3D view of your route.
3. Prepare route cards.
4. Calculate walk duration.
5. Assess height gain and descent.
6. Save your routes.
7. Overlay aerial photographs.
8. Upload routes into (or from) a GPS unit.
9. Print off maps.
10. Share route information.

Compasses

Compass designs have become quite trendy these days. It seems that even navigation equipment cannot escape the influence of fashion. A wide range of sizes, colours and shapes are now available.

But what does a compass really do, and how does it help you navigate? A good compass is a precise but essentially simple instrument. The compass needle has a pointed end, normally painted red. This end points to Magnetic North.

Remembering this enables you, at a very basic level, to know how you are orientated in relation to the points of a compass, and therefore, the landscape.

Compass basics

N – If you walk following the north needle, you are walking in a northerly direction.

S – Follow the other end of the needle and you are moving in a southerly direction.

E – Walk at a right angle to the right of the north needle and you will be heading east.

W – Walk at a right angle to the left of the north needle to travel west.

Compass bits and pieces

We know about the 'business-end' of a compass – the needle – but what other features do you need to know about?

Here is a summary of compass terminology:

- **Baseplate** – onto which the housing and needle sit.
- **Housing** – the circular ring that displays 0-360 degrees.
- **Orienting lines** – lines displayed on the housing to help line up your compass on your map.
- **Direction of travel arrow** – arrow displayed on the base plate, used to take and follow bearings.
- **Lanyard** – to attach it to your wrist or wear round your neck.
- **Measuring scales** – for measuring distance.
- **Romer scales** – to calculate grid references.

Choosing a compass

What should you look for when buying a compass?

Choose one with:

1. A long base plate – this makes taking bearings easier.
2. A chunky housing – easier to use when wearing gloves.
3. A housing that turns smoothly – for ease and precision.
4. Clear numbers – that you can see in poor visibility.
5. Luminous dial and north pointer – for navigating in the dark.
6. Romer scales – for both 1:25,000 and 1:50,000 maps.
7. A smoothly floating needle – for accuracy.
8. A magnifying glass – to help inspect your map more closely.

Go for the best quality you can afford – and then learn how to use it properly.

Compass care

Compasses are delicate pieces of equipment. They can break or become inaccurate, which is the last thing you want when you are in a situation that requires some nifty navigating.

The needle's accuracy can be affected if it is stored next to batteries, mobile phones, other magnets, or metallic objects. Store your compass away from such items. No-one wants a compass that points in the wrong direction.

Keep your compass easily accessible and in a place that protects it from sudden impacts.

Digital compasses

Digital compasses are available. They can be stand-alone devices or incorporated into other instruments, like GPS units. Whist they make some aspects of compass-use easier, calculating bearings from maps is not possible. Battery failure and technical problems can also occur. The simple elegance of a good quality, standard compass is hard to beat.

Bearings

What is a bearing and how does it help you navigate? A bearing tells you the direction in which to travel, in order to reach your target. Imagine you are standing at the centre of a large clock, which, instead of hours, has degrees around its edge.

A bearing is the angle, in degrees, from north to the direction of your intended target.

- North = 0 degrees
- South = 180 degrees
- West = 270 degrees
- East = 90 degrees

For example, if the point you want to travel to is exactly west of your position, you must travel on a bearing of 270 degrees to reach it.

Compass skills

The ability to take and walk on a bearing is an essential skill when walking in poor visibility. It keeps you on the right track. Also, when following paths, you may be faced with several alternative tracks. Which one do you take? By calculating the bearing of the track you should be following (from your map), you can compare this with the bearings of the alternative tracks. Follow the track that has a bearing matching the one on your map.

Taking a bearing

How do you take a bearing? There are two ways to take a bearing:

1. Take a bearing from your map, then use your compass to follow the bearing to your target.

2. Point your compass at a known feature on the land, then relate it back to your map to ascertain your current position.

The first technique is the one you will use most often. This is described below.

How to take a bearing from your map

To use this method, you must know your current position on your map. This is known as 'fixing your position'. Next, you need to identify, on your map, where you want to travel to – your target.

It helps to lay your map on a flat surface when carrying out this exercise. Lay your compass on your map, then follow these steps to calculate your bearing:

1. Align the edge of your compass over the two points on your map, i.e. your current position and your target.

2. Remember to point the direction of travel arrow towards your target.

3. Rotate the compass housing to align the orienting lines (on the housing) with the map's (Easting) grid lines.

4. Remember that the 'N' on the housing should be pointing towards the top of your map.

5. Read off the 'grid bearing' on the edge of the housing, next to the direction of travel arrow.

Follow magnetic bearing

In order to follow this bearing using your compass, you must convert the grid bearing to a 'magnetic bearing'. To do this, you must take into account magnetic variation.

TOP T!P

Regularly practise taking bearings, so that the skill becomes second nature to you.

Magnetic variation

Magnetic variation is the difference, in degrees, between Magnetic North and Grid North. It is also known as declination. It is normal practice to convert a grid bearing, which you have calculated from your map, into a 'magnetic bearing' you follow using your compass.

Once you have worked out magnetic variation, do you add it or subtract it from your grid bearing? There is an easy way to remember this: because the land is much bigger than your map, the magnetic bearing needs to be bigger too.

In practice, this means that you must turn your compass housing to increase the bearing displayed. For example, if your grid bearing is 200 degrees and the magnetic variation is 3 degrees, then you adjust your housing to read 203 degrees. This is the bearing you then follow.

FASCINATING FACT

Magnetic North varies with place and time. The legend on your map will tell you by how many degrees Magnetic North varies from Grid North.

Walking on a bearing

Once you have worked out your bearing, the next step is to walk following this bearing for the required distance, in order to reach your target.

1. Hold your compass correctly

Hold the base plate of your compass firmly in your hand, with the direction of travel arrow pointing away from you. Hold your compass in front of you at the top of your chest. Keep your elbow tucked into the side of your chest to ensure your arm is stable.

2. Working out which way to go

Once you have your magnetic bearing dialled into your compass, leave your housing set.

To find the direction in which to travel, rotate your body until the red end of your compass needle aligns with the north position on the compass housing. The direction of travel arrow on your compass is now pointing along your bearing. Follow this.

3. Following your magnetic bearing

In good visibility, the easiest way to follow a bearing is to pick out a feature that lies on your bearing, and walk towards it. Once you get to it, you repeat the process.

In poor visibility, or at night, there may be no visible features. In these circumstances, you must constantly refer to your compass. Hold it at about chest height and walk following the direction of travel arrow, whilst keeping the red end of your compass needle aligned with the north position on the compass housing.

Take extra care when following bearings in strong side-winds or on slopes – it is easy to drift off course.

Reached your target?

Walking on a bearing is one thing. But how do you know you have arrived at your target? If visibility is good, and you have chosen an easily recognisable feature, you are likely to see your target. It is a different matter when visibility is poor. So, what do you do?

First – some background

In 1892, Naismith, a Scottish mountaineer, devised a simple formula for predicting the time taken to complete a hillwalking route. He explained that people walk 3 miles per hour, and took an additional 30 minutes for every 1000 feet of ascent. This has become known as Naismith's Rule.

Naismith's Rule

Converted to metric, this works out as:

- 5 kilometres per hour.
- Plus an additional 30 minutes per 300 metres of ascent (10 minutes per 100 metres).

This is now a widely used rule-of-thumb for navigators, but must be used with some caution. It assumes a good level of fitness. For those people of average fitness, or carrying heavy rucksacks, or walking in difficult conditions, Naismith's calculations should be regarded as ambitious.

A more conservative formula

Here is a more conservative formula, for people of average fitness walking in good conditions.

- 4 kilometres per hour.
- Plus an additional 36 minutes per 300 metres of ascent (12 minutes per 100 metres).

This can be used as a guide when using walking time as a means of working out distance travelled. For greater accuracy, you should calculate your own walking speed.

Using timing to calculate distance travelled

- You will have previously worked out your walking speed over similar terrain to that which you now intend to travel over on your walk.

- Measure the distance on your map, together with any ascent, from your current location to your target.
- Based on your normal walking speed, calculate how long it should take to reach your target.
- Walk for this amount of time to reach your target.

TOP T!P

Your watch is an important navigational tool. Watches with a 'timer' function are a useful aid for navigators.

Timing chart example

Distance in metres	Time taken based on walking speed of 4 kph
100	1 min 30 sec
200	3 mins
400	6 mins
600	9 mins
800	11 mins
1 kilometre	15 mins
2 kilometres	30 mins
4 kilometres	60 mins

Adding time for ascent

Extra time must be added to your estimates, to take into account any vertical ascent.

Metres of ascent	100	200	400	600	800	1000
Extra time to be added	12 mins	24 mins	48 mins	1 hour 12 mins	1 hour 36 mins	2 hours

Using the timing chart

For example, to travel 1 kilometre on land, whilst making 100 metres of ascent, takes 27 minutes, i.e. 15 minutes to travel the linear distance plus an additional 12 minutes to ascend the vertical height.

TOP T!P

Aim to walk at a steady, comfortable pace, which allows you to travel without having to make to many rest stops.

Using pacing to calculate distance travelled

Pacing can also be used to measure distance covered. To use this method:

- You will need to have previously calculated how many double paces you take to cover one hundred metres – in similar terrain to that over which you now intend to travel.
- Measure the distance on your map, from your current location to your target.
- Based on your pacing, calculate how many double paces are required to reach your target.
- Walk for this number of paces to reach your target.

Draw up your own timing and pacing charts, and take them with you. (Blank charts are shown on pages 182–183)

TOP T!P

To calculate your pace count – use your map to find a 100-metre distance you can clearly identify on land. Walk this distance several times to work out how many double paces you take to cover the ground. To count your paces, add 'one' to your tally each time your right leg hits the ground

Pacing chart

The chart shows a range of paces (from 60 – 80) required to cover 100 metres, together with the equivalent number of paces needed to cover 75, 50 and 25 metres.

100 m	75 m	50 m	25 m
60	45	30	15
65	49	33	17
70	53	35	18
75	56	38	19
80	60	40	20

Using the Pacing Chart

Let's assume that you take 70 paces per 100 metres. Look down the 100 metre column until you see 70, then slide your finger horizontally to find out how many paces you would take to cover 75, 50 or 25 metres. Easy!

Example (a) – if you need to cover a distance of 75 metres, it will take you 53 paces.

Example (b) – If you want to pace 400 metres, don't count 280 paces – it's hard to keep count when you are tired or the weather is poor. Instead, count four lots of 70 paces.

TOP T!P

Attach plastic toggles to your compass lanyard to use as counters. Each time you travel 100 metres, slide a toggle down the cord. This will make keeping count of your distance travelled much easier.

Using timing or pacing

Use timing for longer distances between your position and your target location and pacing for shorter distances, when precision is important.

Timing and pacing are essential skills for navigators. They must be practised in order for them to become second nature. Good navigators make mental adjustments, to adapt their calculations to different terrain and conditions.

Global Positioning Systems – GPS

GPS units (Global Positioning Systems) were originally developed for military purposes but are now widely used by walkers. These units use signals from satellites orbiting the earth to pinpoint position. They can be used anywhere the unit can receive satellite signals. Units can identify positions with an accuracy of up to 3 metres.

How does a GPS help you navigate?

1. Your GPS unit displays your position in the form of a grid reference – ideal when you want to fix your position.

2. You can upload (or key-in) your intended route as a series of 'waypoints', which you can then follow. The unit displays a direction of travel arrow, which you follow from waypoint to waypoint, until your route is completed.

3. As you walk, you can record your route as a 'track' or as a series of plotted waypoints. This can be stored in the unit and used as a route in the future. You can also use this method to backtrack, when necessary.

GPS features

Your GPS unit may also incorporate:

- Electronic compass.

- Altimeter.

- Walking speed display.
- Extended battery life.
- Base maps.
- Colour screen.
- Proximity alarms.
- Sunrise and sunset displays.

Buying a GPS

GPS units vary considerably in price. Expect to pay more for units with colour screens and a large memory (which allows base maps to be uploaded and numerous routes to be stored within them). The ability to connect the GPS to your PC via a USB connection is a useful feature. Units that include altimeters, which use barometric pressure, are regarded as being the most accurate, and are, therefore, more expensive.

Caring for your GPS

Most units are robust but can be damaged by a heavy impact. When not in use, store them in a place that won't come into contact with the ground should you stumble.

Using your GPS

Before heading out with your GPS, check that it has a fresh set of batteries installed and always carry a spare set with you. Take several sets of batteries on multi-day walks and when you are in areas where you cannot buy new ones easily. Get to know your unit's anticipated battery life.

If your GPS cannot pick up a signal from sufficient satellites, it cannot function properly. In areas where the GPS cannot 'see' the sky, such as under heavy tree canopies, close to cliff faces, etc., your unit may temporarily stop functioning.

TOP T!P

Always take a map and compass with you, should something go wrong with your GPS.

It is worth noting, too, that your GPS simply directs you from one waypoint to the next. It cannot identify any hazards that may lie between them. That's your job. Input your waypoints with care, being aware of any obstacles that could lie between them, and be vigilant when using your GPS to navigate.

INFO

Some GPS models can now display detailed OS maps on their screens.

Altimeters

An altimeter is a device that uses air pressure to calculate altitude. Using the principle that air pressure reduces as you ascend, it uses this to work out your height above sea level.

Altimeters help you to navigate. Knowing your altitude can help pinpoint your position. You can also set the altimeter alarm to activate at a predetermined altitude. Simply key-in an altitude at which you want the alarm to sound. This is useful if you want to be prompted to make a change of direction in poor visibility. For example, to be prompted to follow a new path, which as you see from your map, diverts from your route at a certain altitude.

Air pressure changes

Altimeters are not only affected by differences in air pressure due to changes in altitude; changes in weather pressure systems affect them too. If you remain at a set altitude, any changes in air pressure will alter the unit's altitude reading. If this happens, you must recalibrate the unit by reentering the correct altitude before using it again.

Choosing an altimeter

Look for altimeters with large, easy-to-read displays – essential in poor visibility and harsh weather conditions. Many altimeters are worn on the wrist and can also be used as conventional watches. A thermometer is often incorporated into the altimeter, but it has to be attached to something other than your wrist or it will read your body temperature. Try securing it to a visible part of your rucksack instead.

FASCINATING FACT

Altimeters also display air pressure trends, which can be used as a weather forecasting tool.

Pedometers

A pedometer is a small device that counts the number of steps you take. A motion sensor in the pedometer registers your body's vertical movements, and then displays them on a digital display. Some convert your steps into distances, once you have entered your stride length. To function properly, pedometers are normally clipped onto your belt or waistband whilst walking.

Pedometers are popular. Many health organisations use them to encourage people to walk more, and offer them free or on loan. They have been useful in motivating people to walk the recommended 10,000 steps per day.

Be very cautious if you are considering using pedometers for navigating. They can be inaccurate. The sensor can register 'steps' with body movement other than walking motion, and, on changing terrain, your stride length varies too, leading to a miscalculation of the distance covered.

Navigating without a compass or GPS

If you need to navigate and you haven't got a compass or GPS, there are other ways to help you find your way.

Using the sun to navigate

Stick and stone technique

For thousands of years, Man has used the sun to navigate. There are simple ways of identifying direction using the sun's position as a guide. The first technique depends on the sun being strong enough to cast a shadow, so ensure that you use it in an open area of level ground.

To use the 'stick and stone' technique, plant a straight stick in the ground vertically. Use one of at least three feet (90 cm) in length. Look for the shadow of the stick on the ground, then place a stone accurately on the end of the shadow. Then wait for 20 minutes. Because the sun moves during this time, the shadow it casts moves too. Place another stone on the end of the new shadow. Draw a line on the ground from one stone to the next. Then draw another at 90 degrees to this.

The line between the stones runs approximately east to west, the other line runs north to south. Place your left foot next to the first stone and your right next to the second stone. You are now facing north, with your back towards south. To your left is west and to your right is east.

Watch technique

To use this technique, you need a watch with hands. If you only have a digital watch, you can mimic this method by drawing a watch face on a piece of paper. In the UK, your watch must be set to GMT, or, if using the technique abroad, to local time with no changes for summer time.

Northern hemisphere

In the northern hemisphere, point the hour hand of your watch in the direction of the sun. (Use a small twig to cast a shadow, rather than having to stare at the sun.) Bisect the angle between the hour hand and 12 o'clock on your watch. This line runs south/north. The end aiming away from the sun is north. From this, you can plot west/east lines.

Southern hemisphere

Aim 12 o'clock on your watch in the direction of the sun. Then bisect the angle between 12 o'clock and the hour hand of your watch. The end of this line, nearest the sun, is pointing north.

Using the Moon to indicate direction

Crescent moon

The moon can be used to indicate direction, too. You can use the first and last quarters of the moon's phases to give an approximate direction for south, in the northern hemisphere, and north in the southern hemisphere.

To use this method, draw an imaginary line through each tip of the crescent, and continue this line towards the horizon. Where the line crosses the horizon, that is approximately south.

Full moon

Throughout the night, the full moon passes through different parts of the sky. It follows a set pattern. The full moon's position (in the UK) at different times during the night is shown in the following table:

Time	Moon's position
6pm	East
9pm	Southeast
Midnight	South
3am	Southeast
6am	South

Navigating by the stars

The North Star

The North Star (Polaris) has been used to identify direction for thousands of years in the northern hemisphere. A clear night and a knowledge of its position in the sky is needed in order to use this technique.

To locate the North Star, look for a constellation of stars known as The Plough (or Big Dipper or The Great Bear). Draw an imaginary line through the two stars that make up the last part of the 'handle' of the Plough. Follow this line for about six times the distance of the two stars. The star in the sky at this point is the North Star.

To get a better 'fix' on the North Star, use another constellation, Cassiopeia, together with The Plough. Cassiopeia is a 'W' shaped group of stars located opposite The Plough. The North Star is located midway between the two constellations.

Trees as an indication of direction

Trees can be used as a very approximate guide to direction. They tend to have more foliage and branch growth on the side that receives the most sun, i.e. a southerly direction in the northern hemisphere.

Moss prefers to grow in damp, shady conditions. It tends to grow on the north side of trees in the northern hemisphere, which are hidden from the sun.

In the UK, the prevailing winds come from the south west. In open country, trees may grow bending away from these winds. But be aware that local winds also sculpt tree growth, and these may be channelled from other directions.

TOP T!P

Familiarise yourself with the main constellations by using a star chart. These are relatively inexpensive to buy.

Getting Lost

“We’re not lost. We’re locationally challenged.”

John M. Ford
Writer and poet (1957—2006)

Chapter 8

Getting Lost

Lost

Most walkers will be 'locationally challenged' at one time or another. The epic detour you made after getting lost may appear laughable once you are safely home, but not whilst you are struggling to find your way.

Getting lost happens for a variety of reasons. The main ones being lack of concentration or the effects of weather conditions. It is easy to overlook the path you should have taken whilst chatting with friends; clouds may descend, which limits visibility; footpaths can become obscured by snow.

Using GPS to fix your position, if you are carrying a GPS unit and you know how to use it, you can identify your position with the click of a couple of buttons. (See the section on GPS, pages 113–115). If you are not carrying a GPS, you don't know how to use it, or your batteries have died, you need to find other ways to get you back on the right track.

TOP T!P

Avoid walking in weather conditions or over types of terrain beyond your capabilities as a navigator.

What does getting lost feel like?

Getting lost is most likely to occur towards the end of your day's walk, when you may be feeling cold, tired and hungry. You are likely to experience some or all of these feelings:

- Uneasy at first.
- Frustrated.
- Angry.
- Under pressure.
- Scared.

Your response will vary according to your circumstances. Getting lost on a low level footpath in summer is very different from losing your way in treacherous terrain in a howling winter's gale.

What you should do first

1. Sit down in a sheltered spot.
2. Note the time.
3. Have something to eat and drink.
4. Tell yourself that you will be OK

FASCINATING FACT

Your brain works more effectively when you are calm and not hungry or dehydrated.

Your brain needs information

To work out where you are, your brain needs information. Piece together all the clues, just as a detective would. Become the Hercule Poirot of the outdoors. Gather clues…

- What can you see around you?
- Where have you been?
- How much time has passed since your last 'fix' (last known location)?

If you can see features on the land...

- Set your map, using your compass.
- Can you match features on your map with what you see?
- Can you get a better view higher up or lower down?
- If you have an altimeter, what is your altitude?
- Beware of 'making' features fit.
- Take bearings of any linear features that are around you, e.g. footpaths, walls and rivers.
- Look at contours and the shape of the land.

If you cannot see anything that helps

Maybe you are on featureless terrain, or paths are obscured by snow, or you can't see due to weather or darkness.

- What information do you have?
- What can you obtain?

Gather more facts...

- Where was your last 'fix'?
- How long ago was it?
- What has the terrain been like since?
- In which direction were you walking?
- Can you obtain more clues by walking for another 10 minutes?

Retrace your steps?

If time and conditions allow, retracing your steps may be an option worth considering. By doing so, you might identify where you went astray and can get back on course. You may decide to retrace your steps for a set period of time – say 5 or 10 minutes. If this doesn't help, you will have to think of other ways to get back on course.

Alternatively, you could retrace your whole route and return to your start point. But, before retracing your steps, consider:

- Whether you can clearly identify the way you came.
- How long it will take you to return by this route.
- The weather conditions.
- Hours of remaining daylight.
- The terrain over which you are intending to return.
- Your own (and other group member's) physical condition.
- The alternatives that are open to you.

Area of probability

If you have insufficient information to get a firm fix on your position, you should work out an 'area of probability' in which you are located. It is better than nothing.

- Calculate the distance you could have covered since your last fix.
  - Use the timing chart as a guide.
  - How far could you have gone – maximum and minimum?
- Draw the extent of this area on your map.

If you have located your position

- Plot a new route to your objective, same route, or revised route.

If you have not located your position

Use your compass to travel on a bearing from your area of probability to a 'collecting feature'. These are large, linear features, which you can be certain of hitting when travelling on a bearing towards them. Examples are major rivers and roads. Once reached, you can then make your way back to your destination. Continue to look for more clues as you travel, which may help you fix your position.

Follow streams and rivers to habitation

Another strategy is to follow streams and rivers downstream, on the basis that you will eventually reach habitation. Before doing so, you must realise that:

- It may be a long way.
- It may be hazardous and steep.
- Once habitation is reached, you will have to find a way of returning to your planned destination.

Safety

Whichever strategy you choose, safety is paramount.

- Assess the risks.
- Work out a plan.
- It will take more time.
- It will take concentration.

- If possible, contact your responsible person a.s.a.p. Tell them of your revised plans and that you are likely to be late. Keep them updated and let them know when you are back safely.

TOP T!P

Make sure your mobile phone, whistle and torch are easily accessible, in case of an emergency, and that your phone is fully charged and your torch has new, or reasonably new, batteries.

Staying put

If making progress puts you in danger, such as walking in extreme weather conditions or trying to cross hazardous terrain in poor visibility, the safest option may be to stay put until conditions improve.

When you become stationary, you can become cold very quickly. Ensure that you find a sheltered spot and put on all your spare clothing. For wilderness and mountain walks, carry an emergency shelter or lightweight bivvy bag for such unexpected eventualities.

Calling for help in an emergency

Only call mountain rescue if there is an emergency. If you or one of your party is ill or injured, or if there is a serious threat to your safety, then make the call (See the next chapter for more details).

Don't rely on mobile phones working in remote areas. There is often no signal. If you are unable to use your phone to call for help, then you will have to shout or use a distress signal to attract attention (See the next chapter for more details).

Better Safe than Sorry

"Nobody trips over mountains. It is the small pebble that causes you to stumble."

Unknown

Chapter 9
Better Safe than Sorry

Don't become a statistic

Walking is a very safe activity. Millions of walkers enjoy their pastime each week, and only a fraction of incidents and accidents occur. But, however safe, it does pay to plan your walk with safety in mind and adopt a common-sense approach to your walking trips.

You should be aware of potential hazards that can affect the safety and enjoyment of your walk. A little forethought and preparedness is all that is needed. Don't become a statistic. No-one really wants to bring grapes to your hospital bed.

Escape routes

When planning walks in mountainous terrain, build an escape route into your plan, in case of an emergency or deteriorating weather conditions. Where possible, pick out an alternative route that provides a speedy, safe return to your start point. Make a note of your escape route on your route planner.

The weather

Weather in the UK is very changeable, so we need to take extra care when we plan our walking trips. Weather conditions may mean we have to adjust or curtail our plans. Severe weather conditions can make routes unsafe, reduce morale, slow progress, and sap energy.

Always check conditions before you depart, and don't be embarrassed about changing your plans if necessary. Bear in mind that conditions at higher altitudes are likely to be much more severe than at lower levels.

Special considerations in mountainous areas

Lapse rate

Typically, air temperature reduces as you ascend. This temperature difference is known as the lapse rate. The rate varies according to whether the air is dry or saturated.

- **Dry air** – temperature reduces by 1 degree C for each 100 metres of ascent.
- **Saturated air** – temperature reduces by 1 degree C for each 200 metres of ascent.

Wind speed

Wind speed is often greater at higher altitudes. This is due to wind being funnelled between mountain summits and the lowest part of the Earth's atmosphere – the troposphere. Wind speed increases as the air is squeezed through. Air is also forced between mountains, which causes a localised increase in wind speed. Wind direction depends on how the air has been channelled through the landscape *(See the Beaufort Scale of Wind Speeds on page 184).*

FASCINATING FACT

Highest gust record: 150 knots (173 miles per hour) Cairngorm (1,245 metres), 20 March 1986.

Windchill

The windchill temperature is the temperature it feels like outside, based on the effects of wind speed and air temperature. It is based on the rate of heat loss from exposed skin. As the wind increases, the body is cooled at a faster rate, causing the skin temperature to drop.

Though there are several windchill charts in use, this is the one that the Met Office uses. Windspeed is shown in the left-hand column and air temperature across the top. The other figures are the windchill temperatures.

	5°C	**0°C**	**-5°C**	**-10°C**	**-15°C**
10mph	2°C	-5°C	-11°C	-17°C	-23°C
20mph	0°C	-7°C	-13°C	-20°C	-26°C
30mph	-1°C	-8°C	-15°C	-22°C	-28°C
40mph	-2°C	-9°C	-16°C	-23°C	-30°C

Cloud and precipitation

When air is forced over higher ground, it cools as it rises. As the air is cooled below its dewpoint, tiny droplets of moisture are formed and clouds are created. This is why cloud and mist are often associated with mountainous areas. You knew there was a good reason to buy that expensive waterproof jacket.

Rain is formed inside clouds when supercooled cold water meets particles of dust, salt or sand, forming ice crystals. The ice crystals provide a nucleus onto which more water droplets attach, increasing the size of the droplet or, in colder air, snowflakes. When the droplet or snowflake becomes large enough, it falls as rain or snow.

Hailstones are formed from ice crystals or frozen raindrops, which are swept upwards through the cloud to gain several layers of ice. This process may occur several times before they are finally heavy enough to fall out of the cloud.

Conditions underfoot

Low temperatures in mountainous areas result in ice and snow remaining on the ground, even when there are no signs of it in the valleys. Snow cover can remain on the highest Scottish mountains even in mid summer. In other parts of the world, snow is ever present at higher altitudes. Local outdoor retailers are often the best source of information for seasonal mountaintop conditions.

Thunderstorms

Each year, an estimated 100,000 people throughout the world are injured and 10,000 people are killed by lightning – more than killed in hurricanes, tornadoes or floods. Lightning tends to strike high points, so walking on mountaintops and ridges in a thunderstorm is potentially dangerous. The safest option is to head for lower ground.

To estimate how far away a thunderstorm is from you, count the number of seconds from the lightning flash to the sound of thunder. Divide this number by three. This tells you how far away the storm is, in kilometres.

Repeat this procedure to work out whether the storm is approaching or moving away.

- If the time between lightning and thunder is decreasing – the storm is approaching.
- If the time between lightning and thunder is increasing – the storm is moving away.

Other hazards

Steep terrain

When planning journeys across steep ground, research the route to ensure it is within your capabilities. Check for escape routes. Plan to climb steep ground early in your walk, whilst your legs are fresh. When descending steep terrain, travel carefully and do not rush. Focus on where you are placing your feet, and avoid distractions that could result in you slipping or tripping. Many accidents happen when descending footpaths on tired legs.

River crossings

Wading across rivers should only be done as a last resort.

TOP T!P

Before making a long descent, eat a high carbohydrate snack to give you some extra energy.

Always choose to use a bridge, even if this means a detour. The power of a river is easily underestimated, and a fast-flowing river does not need to be very deep to topple you over. Getting soaked increases the risk of hypothermia. Unseen, deep pools, obstacles and slippery river beds also makes river crossing a hazardous activity.

If you are forced to make a river crossing:

- Look for a straight, shallow section of river with an even river bed.
- Check that there are no downstream dangers or obstacles.
- Look for low banks that are easy to ascend and descend.
- Loosen rucksack straps and belts.
- Use a walking pole, branch, or other people for support.
- Wring out any wet clothes; start walking soon afterwards, to keep warm, and eat high energy snacks.

FRIGHTENING FACT

When surrounded by cold water, the body cools 30 times faster than in dry air.

Boggy ground and quicksand

Boggy ground and quicksand can trap unsuspecting walkers. Avoid problems by staying on waymarked routes and clearly-defined footpaths in these areas.

Rockfall

Rocks can be dislodged by people and animals. Rocks also fracture as a result of freezing and thawing of ice within their cracks. The ground at rockfall areas is often littered with rocks from previous falls. Avoid camping in these areas and pass through them quickly. If you dislodge a rock yourself, or see rockfall that may endanger others, shout a warning.

Avalanches

Avalanches have injured and claimed the lives of people in many of the mountainous areas of the UK. The recent spate of mild winters has limited snowfall levels and reduced avalanche risks in many places. The Scottish peaks, being higher and subject to different weather fronts, have much more snowfall, and avalanches occur regularly. The Sport Scotland Avalanche Information Service publish daily forecasts of the avalanche, snow, and climbing conditions at five climbing areas in Scotland, throughout the winter season.

> **INFO**
>
> www.sais.gov.uk provides useful information about avalanches and how to avoid them.

Bulls in fields

Section 59 of the Wildlife & Countryside Act 1981 bans the keeping of bulls in fields crossed by a right-of-way, except if they are:

- under the age of 10 months; or

- not of a recognised dairy breed, provided they are accompanied by cows or heifers.

'Recognised dairy breeds' are defined as the following: Ayrshire, British Friesian, British Holstein, Dairy Shorthorn, Guernsey, Jersey, and Kerry. Typically, bulls from these breeds are more unpredictable and aggressive.

“Everywhere is within walking distance if you have the time.”

Steven Wright
US comedian and actor (1955—)

Cows and bullocks

There have been a number of incidents where walkers have been trampled by cows or bullocks. Most of these have been walkers with dogs crossing fields containing cows with their calves. The cows appear to have been 'protecting' their young. Here are some useful tips from the Ramblers Association, to help avoid trouble:

- If you feel threatened, find an alternative route.
- Keep your dog under close control, but let go of the lead and allow your dog to run away, if a cow or bull starts to act aggressively.
- Walk quietly around a herd and avoid splitting groups of cattle.
- If cattle start to walk towards you, carry on and do not run.
- If a bull or cow comes up very close, turn round to face it, waving your arms and shouting loudly.
- Report any serious incidents to the landowner, Highways Authority, and the Health & Safety Executive.

First aid

First aid courses

Attend a good first aid course. You will learn valuable skills and gain confidence in dealing with emergency situations and injuries. Some training organisations offer courses with an emphasis on the outdoors. These are particularly useful if you want to be equipped to deal with injuries and incidents that occur whilst walking.

It is important to keep your skills up-to-date; many courses issue certificates that must be renewed every 3 years, by attending a requalification course.

First aid in practice

Here are some basic guidelines for dealing with injuries and incidents. These are not necessarily up-to-date or definitive treatments and shouldn't be relied upon. You can obtain comprehensive details from a qualified first aid trainer, up-to-date first aid books, or via the NHS Direct website www.nhsdirect.nhs.uk

Blisters

The unbroken skin over a blister provides a natural barrier to infection. Keeping blisters intact and unbroken will help avoid infection – so never pierce a blister with a needle. As new skin grows beneath the blister, the fluid within it will be reabsorbed by your body, and the skin on top will dry out and peel off.

- Cover small blisters with a plaster or other 'blister' dressings.
- Cover large blisters with a gauze pad or dressing and secure it with tape.
- If you have a blister in a position that is causing you pain, or that makes it likely to burst, shield it with a pad of soft, absorbent dressing.
- If a blister bursts, don't peel off the skin. Press the area to remove the fluid inside, then cover the blister with a dry, sterile dressing to protect it from infection until it heals.

TOP T!P

Prevention is better than a cure. Stop as soon as you feel a hot-spot developing on your foot and attend to it before it becomes a blister.

Sprains and strains

Sprains are injuries to joints, where ligaments have been stretched or partially torn. Strains are tearing injuries to muscles or tendons. Symptoms include pain, swelling and stiffness around the affected area.

Treat with R-I-C-E-S.

- **R** – Rest
- **I** – Apply ice (wrapped in cloth) or a cold water compress.
- **C** – Compression. Apply a firm elastic bandage until the swelling starts to go down.
- **E** – Elevate the injured limb.
- **S** – Stabilise with a light splint.

Ankle and lower leg injuries

If the area is very swollen and unable to bear any weight, treat it as a broken bone. Totally immobilise the area with a splint and ensure that the casualty is insulated from the ground and kept warm. Arrange for the casualty to be evacuated.

Ticks

Lyme disease is carried by the sheep tick, which also feeds on deer. Ticks also like to chomp on unsuspecting walkers, and the disease can be passed on to them through a bite. Common symptoms include – generally feeling unwell, flu-like symptoms, tiredness, muscle pain, weakness, joint pain, and headaches. In some cases, an expanding 'bull's eye' shaped rash appears on the skin at the site of the tick bite.

To avoid being bitten, wear long trousers and long sleeved shirts when walking in areas where ticks may be present. Check yourself (and dogs if they have been walking with you) for ticks after your walk. They are small and difficult to see at first, but grow, becoming lighter in colour as they gorge on blood.

To remove them:

- Grasp the tick as close to the skin as possible without squeezing the tick's body, pull firmly and steadily. Use tweezers, a cotton thread around the tick's mouthparts, or a tick removal tool (available from vets and pet shops). Wash and clean the bite area with an antiseptic.

INFO

Ticks prefer to live in moist, shady areas, such as grass, bracken and leaf litter, and are most active between April and October.

Hypothermia

Hypothermia is a condition where the normal body temperature of 37°C (98.6°F) drops below 35° (95°F). This is a potentially life-threatening condition and should be taken very seriously.

Symptoms of hypothermia are characterised by 'umbles'. Watch out for anyone displaying the following signs.

Grumbles – Fumbles – Mumbles – Stumbles – Tumbles

Treat the casualty by:

- Sheltering them from the elements.
- Insulating them from the ground.
- Replacing any wet clothing.
- Adding extra layers and/or putting them inside a survival bag or sleeping bag.

- Giving them warm drinks and high energy foods (no alcohol).
- Reassuring them.
- Evacuating them for medical treatment when they are rewarmed and stable.

First aid kits

Invest in a good first aid kit. For short, low level walks, a small, basic kit may be all that you need. Take a comprehensive first aid kit with you if you are walking in wild and mountainous areas, or if trekking abroad. Good kits are available from major outdoor retailers.

- Keep your kit accessible.
- Keep it dry.
- Know what it contains and how to use it.

Mountain rescue

The UK's popular walking and climbing areas are covered by mountain rescue teams. They are called out in all weather conditions, at any time of the day, to help people who are in difficulty. Teams are made up of volunteers, who give up their time and put themselves at risk for the good of others. They are the unsung heros of the outdoors. Use the mountain rescue service only in an emergency or if your safety is at risk. Be aware that it may be many hours before mountain rescue is able to locate you.

Reporting an incident

Mountain rescue can be contacted by phoning 999 and asking for the mountain rescue service. Provide the operator with a grid reference and description of your location. It is good practice to carry an accident report form, onto which you can write all the key information about an incident, the casualty and your location. Good outdoor first aid kits often include these.

MOUNTAIN
RESCUE
AMBULANCE
WASDALE MOUNTAIN
RESCUE TEAM

This makes passing on these details to the operator much easier. Stay by the phone, so that mountain rescue can contact you again if they need to.

TOP T!P

So that you can find it easily, attach your whistle to the lanyard of your compass.

Distress signals

The international distress signal is six blows of a whistle or flashes of a light, made in quick succession. Then repeated at one minute intervals.

Self-reliance

It is good to become self-reliant in the outdoors. Being skilled and confident helps you make better decisions, avoid potential problems, and handle difficult situations. Become more self-reliant by:

- Attending outdoor training courses.
- Reading books and buying DVDs to develop your skills.
- Regularly practising your techniques.
- Applying your skills in unfamiliar areas.
- Teaching others.

INFO

Mountain Rescue teams rely on donations to fund their activities. Make a donation when you see one of their collection boxes. You never know when you might need them to get you out of trouble.

Backpacking

“The true traveller is he who goes on foot, and even then, he sits down a lot of the time.”

Colette, Paris from My Window, 1944
French novelist (1873—1954)

Chapter 10
Backpacking

Backpacking

Backpacking is the closest you get to being a nomad. Carrying your belongings on your back, plodding from place to place, setting up camp for the night, then moving on to pastures new. It gives you greater flexibility to explore the landscape and, once you have bought your kit, it is cheaper than paying for accommodation for the night. You carry your bed and breakfast on your back!

The secret to enjoyable backpacking is keeping the weight in your rucksack to the bare minimum. Use the lightest gear and leave the unimportant things behind. Some people take ultralight backpacking to the extreme, by snapping the handle off their toothbrush to cut down on unnecessary weight. This may be a little radical, but scrutinise your kit and throw out those unwanted pounds. It is important, if you don't want the weight of the world on your shoulders.

Camping

There is nothing quite like the smell of bacon sizzling on a camp stove in the morning. But then it has to be good to coax you out of your cosy sleeping bag and into the cold morning air. A breakfast bacon butty and mug of hot tea is truly savoured when you are camping. There is nothing quite like it.

Camping takes you back to more primitive days. To times when our ancestors sat outside their caves, cooking a wild boar over an open fire (for their wild boar butty). It strips away our modern day luxuries and gets us back to the essentials – food, shelter, and preferably a convenient pub.

Campsites

You can find campsites in all the popular walking destinations. In the UK, most of them are shown on Ordnance Survey maps as a small blue tent symbol. Tourist Information Centres have lists of sites, and an internet search will turn up many useful camping websites. Word of mouth recommendations are best, so ask other walkers for their favourite sites.

Facilities

Standards vary widely. Some offer basic facilities – a place to pitch your tent, a toilet, and a cold tap. Others offer hot showers, club houses and campsite shops. The most popular campsites can be busy all year round, particularly in hardcore walking areas. You may have to book a pitch in advance to secure your place, particularly in high season.

Prices

Camping prices are charged in different ways – sometimes based on the number of people, and/or per tents. You may also have to pay for car parking, and showers are often operated on a coin meter. Overall, expect to pay approximately one third of the price of a standard Bed & Breakfast per person, per night.

TOP T!P

Pitch your tent away from shower and toilet blocks, for less noise and better quality air!

Annoyances

Some campsites are noisy places, which can be frustrating if you are trying to get a early night after a hard walk. Take a pair of earplugs with you to help you get a good night's sleep.

Be aware that campsites next to rivers and streams flood on occasion. Tents have been known to start floating in the night after a huge downpour. Pitch your tent on higher ground, away from running water where possible. This also reduces the number of midges and mozzies that will buzz around your tent.

Going Wild

It's good to go wild. If you don't like the idea of campsites, and prefer solitude and great views, then pitch your tent in the middle of nowhere – it gives you a real sense of what the outdoors is all about. Wild camping is a wonderful experience. But before you rush out for a spot of wild camping, there are legal and environmental issues.

Legal Issues

England and Wales

There is no legal right to camp in the wild and you may be trespassing by doing so. However, wild camping is often informally tolerated in many upland areas.

Scotland

The Land Reform (Scotland) Act 2003 and Scottish Outdoor Access Code establish a statutory right to camp in the wild. The Code describes your responsibilities and best practice, which should be followed when exercising your right to camp wild.

INFO

Find more details at www.outdooraccess-scotland.com

Wild campcraft

- Pitch near a supply of clean, running water (but be aware of potential flooding).
- Beware of falling branches.
- Designated toilet areas should be at least 60 metres (200 feet) from water.
- Camp as unobtrusively as possible, away from habitation.
- Don't stay in the same spot for more than 3 days, as this damages vegetation.
- Carry out everything you carried in, including food scraps.
- Use a stove rather than lighting a fire.

Tents

Tents for backpacking

When backpacking, your tent is your bulkiest and heaviest piece of equipment. Take the smallest, lightest tent you can get hold of. It should also be easy to pitch and strong enough to withstand the kind of weather conditions in which you will be camping. If you intend to camp in high, remote areas, you must have a good quality tent that is built for harsh weather conditions. Poor quality tents are flattened at relatively low wind speeds.

Season ratings

Like boots, tents are categorised in 'season' ratings. If you are intending to use your tent in adverse weather conditions, or in mountainous areas, choose a four season tent.

Important features

- Low pack size.
- Low weight.
- Integral groundsheet.
- Insect netting (small enough to keep out midges).
- Large porch area.
- Colour coded poles.
- Internal vents (to reduce condensation).
- Internal pockets and hanging clips.
- Streamlined design.

Tent sizes

Tents are labelled with size details, e.g. a '2 man tent' has sufficient internal space for two occupants. An extended porch area provides useful space for storing equipment.

Pitching

Practise pitching your tent before using it for the first time in the outdoors. Struggling to pitch your tent on a campsite full of people can be humiliating. You may have to pitch your tent in the dark and in bad weather conditions. If you are adept at tent pitching, this will not pose a problem.

Sleeping bags

Down or synthetic?

Sleeping bags for backpacking should be light and compact, yet substantial enough to keep you warm. Down-filled bags are the best quality, but are expensive and ineffective when wet. Synthetic-filled bags are less expensive but are heavier and bulky. They perform better when wet and dry quicker than down bags.

Size and features

Choose bags to suit your body size; avoid bags that are too big for you, as these waste heat in the voids around your body. Hoods, draw cords, and water retardant outer shells are also very useful features.

Temperature ratings

Check that the bag's temperature rating meets your needs. Look for the 'comfort temperature' – the minimum temperature at which you will be comfortable. These are only a guide and not a guarantee that you will feel warm at these temperatures.

TOP T!P

A fleece or silk liner will keep you warmer and keep the inside of your sleeping bag clean.

Sleeping mats

Sleeping mats insulate your body from the ground temperature and make sleeping more comfortable. Two main types of mat are available – inflatable and compressed foam. Both types can be rolled/folded up when not in use. Three-quarter length versions are good options for backpacking, keeping weight and bulkiness to a minimum. If you use a three-quarter length mat, use your rucksack to insulate your legs from the ground.

TOP T!P

When using an inflatable mat, remember to take a mat repair kit with you, in case it gets punctured.

Stoves

Choosing

If you want hot food and drinks, you will need a lightweight stove. When choosing a stove, you must consider the stove itself and fuel availability. There are many types of stoves. Some operate using only one kind of fuel whilst others are able to use several different types.

Fuel

If you intend to backpack for several days, you may need to obtain new supplies of fuel. Your stove must be able to use the fuel that is locally available. If you want to use your stove overseas, check which type of fuel can be bought at your destination, then make sure your stove is compatible.

Stoves for backpacking in the UK

Backpacking stoves should be small and lightweight and easy to use. These are the most popular types of stove available, ranging from the ultra simple to the slightly more complicated.

- **Army style hexamine**
  - Pros: small, lightweight, uses a fuel block, easy to use.
  - Cons: low heat output, uncontrollable flame, fumes.
- **Trangia**
  - Pros: simple to use, uses methylated spirits as fuel.
  - Cons: bulky, weight of liquid fuel, limited flame control, low heat output.
- **Butane/Propane**
  - Pros: easy to use, uses sealed cartridges, reasonable heat output, controllable flame.
  - Cons: bulky cartridges, needs careful disposal, different types of cartridge fittings.
- **Liquid multi fuel**
  - Pros: fuel availability, heat output.
  - Cons: requires priming, cost.

Ignition

Don't forget to take a box of weatherproof matches, or a windproof lighter, with you, wrapped in plastic bags to prevent water damage. Some stoves have a built-in system that ignites the unit at the click of a button.

Carrying fuel

Carry liquid fuel in a suitable, sturdy container and ensure it is properly labelled. Pack fuel at the bottom of your rucksack, in case the contents leak.

Stove safety

Because of the dangers of carbon monoxide poisoning and the risk of fire, never use a stove inside your tent. Set up your stove in the open, on a level surface outside your tent. Only use the porch area of your tent in severe weather conditions, as this can be dangerous. Tents burn very quickly. If you do so, have a knife easily accessible, which will enable you to cut an emergency exit in your tent if necessary, and a container of water ready for dousing any flames.

Hot food

Food doesn't only provide you with calories and nutrients, it performs an important psychological function, too. Whilst it is possible to just eat cold, ready-cooked food when backpacking, hot food gives you a mental boost, and warms you. The inconvenience of the extra weight of a stove and fuel, and the additional time it takes to prepare hot food, is exceeded by the benefits of having hot food and drinks.

Ready Steady Cook

Walk into any outdoor retailers and you will find a selection of camping meals. These are pre-packed, ready-cooked foods that need to be reheated. Dehydrated versions are lightweight but need water adding prior to heating. Hydrated meals weigh more but can be eaten cold, if necessary – useful if you cannot light your stove for whatever reason.

TOP T!P

Eat 'boil in the bag' meals straight from the packet, rather than emptying the contents onto a plate. This cuts down on the amount of equipment you have to take and the amount of washing-up you have to do.

Make your own

Making your own meals is much less expensive than buying pre-packed ones. Nutritious recipes can be put together quickly and easily by taking a few ingredients with you. Pasta and rice are a good base for many meals. They are quick and easy to cook and are loaded with carbohydrates. Carry food that does not have to be kept chilled, and avoid tinned foods, as these tend to be heavy. If necessary, re-wrap unused food items in low weight packaging.

> **INFO**
> There are several good books available that contain camping and backpacking recipes. Look out for them at your outdoor retailers.

Snacks

Keep them accessible

It is important to keep up your energy levels whilst walking, so take a selection of snacks with you. Make sure that your snacks are easily accessible – fill your pockets. This is especially important in poor weather conditions, when the last thing you feel like doing is stopping and delving into your rucksack to find something to nibble on. A well-timed snack can kick start your mental faculties – helping you with tricky navigation, or motivating you when you need to exert some extra effort. Snacks are also comforting when the weather is bleak. So keep them handy.

Sugar rush

Beware of sugary snacks that provide you with a short-lived boost to your blood sugar. Snacks that gradually release energy into your body, over a longer period, are preferable.

Outdoor Etiquette

“Tread softly because you tread on my dreams.”

William Butler Yeats,
He Wishes for the Cloths of Heaven, 1899
Irish poet and dramatist (1865—1939)

Chapter 11

Outdoor Etiquette

Leave no trace

With the growing interest in outdoor pursuits, it is more important than ever before that we minimise our impact whilst out there. We all want to continue to enjoy the beauty and tranquility of the outdoors, so it is up to us to respect the landscape, its wildlife, and the others who enjoy it too.

Adopt a minimum impact policy when outdoors. Enjoy the outdoors and pass through it gently and quietly, leaving no trace you were ever there. Here are some 'minimum impact' guidelines. Respect other people and allow them to enjoy the outdoors too. Give them their own space and allow them pass you on the path, if they need to. Many people live and work in areas that are popular with walkers. Respect their privacy, and take care not to park your car in areas that may cause them problems.

Litter

Litter, in whatever form, should not be left in the countryside. This includes orange peel, banana skins, cigarette stubs, and tissue paper, which, although biodegradable, can take many years to decompose. A good maxim is to leave nothing but footprints in the countryside.

If you see a discarded plastic bottle or sweet wrapper, pick it up and dispose of it yourself. Then smile and feel good, knowing that you have done your bit for the countryside.

FRIGHTENING FACTS

The average number of years required for these items to biodegrade: orange peel – 2 years, cigarette butt – 3 years, tin can – 80-100 years, aluminium can – 200-400 years.

Fires

Lighting fires is forbidden in many areas. They can easily get out of control and cause lots of damage. In some areas, lighting fires can cause the underlying peat to ignite, which smoulders unnoticed for many days before spreading above ground. Campfires also often leave unsightly, charred scars on the natural landscape.

Although it is sometimes very tempting to light a campfire, because it feels like a very outdoorsy thing to do, stick to using a stove for cooking and light a small lantern or tea lights if you want some atmospheric illumination.

Noise

Many people venture into the countryside to escape into a peaceful environment, so avoid making unnecessary noise.

'Amusing' ring tones and someone hollering into a mobile phone is enough to make many people's blood boil. Ideally, keep your mobile switched off during your walks. If you are expecting an urgent call, set it to vibrate mode and put it in a pocket where you can 'feel' someone calling. Make your calls when you've finished your walk, not when you are on the summit of a favourite peak. Enjoy being inaccessible for a while.

There are few things more frustrating than trying to get to sleep after a hard day's walk, then being kept awake by noisy campsite neighbours. Though many campsites have rules restricting night-time noise, this is sometimes not adhered to, or enforced. We can set an example by sticking to the rules.

Wildlife

One of the joys of being outdoors is seeing wildlife. A fleeting glimpse of a deer or a fox, the sight of a raptor capturing its prey, or trout shimmering in a mountain stream, are wonderful, unforgettable experiences.

Wild creatures are timid and avoid contact with humankind wherever possible. They flee in order to protect themselves. Travelling quietly improves your chances of seeing wildlife.

Dogs or children shouldn't be allowed to chase wild animals, and we should not do anything that might damage the often delicate wild habitats.

TOP T!P

Take a pocket wildlife guidebook and a small pair of binoculars with you on your walks.

"If you are seeking creative ideas, go out walking. Angels whisper to a man when he goes for a walk."

Raymond Inmon
Author

Paths and erosion

Erosion is a major problem in popular walking areas. The impact of hundreds of feet and walking poles causes damage to the land. The scars of footpaths snaking through the landscape are a very visible reminder of this. Thousands of pounds, and countless hours, are spent each year by organisations and individuals repairing footpaths.

We can minimise our impact as walkers by following some advice from the *Fix the Fells* website.

- Place your feet thoughtfully – every single footstep causes wear and tear on the environment.
- Keep to the path surface. Do not walk on the vegetation at the edge of the path.
- Remember that the slow-growing plants that survive on mountains are particularly vulnerable to trampling.
- Do not take shortcuts – other users and water will soon follow your tracks, and an erosion scar will develop.
- Do not build or add to cairns – removing stones from paths can make problems worse.

> **INFO**
> Why not volunteer to help repair footpaths? As well as helping the environment, it's good fun. See: **www.fixthefells.co.uk** and **www.nationaltrust.org.uk**

How to poo in the woods

Human waste should be disposed of properly, not just left behind a bush or boulder. Not only is this offensive to other people, but it can also spread disease, harm wildlife and damage the ecosystem. The following steps help to minimise the impact of human waste and to speed up its decomposition.

If you are likely to be using the great outdoors as a WC, then it helps to be prepared. You will need:

1. A small trowel.
2. A stick.
3. Loo roll or tissues.
4. Plastic bags.
5. Antibacterial wipes.

The procedure:

- Find an area well away from footpaths, and at least 60 metres (200 feet) away from any water sources.
- Look for an area that has rich-looking, organic soil – and dig a hole at least 15 cm (6 inches) deep. Keep a plug of topsoil.
- Use the hole. Then refill it with half of the soil and stir with a stick. Add the remaining soil and then replace the plug of topsoil.
- Don't throw used toilet paper in the hole – double bag it and take it with you.
- Clean your hands with an antibacterial wipe and put it and the packaging in the bag. Wash your hands more thoroughly as soon as possible.

FRIGHTENING FACTS

In some areas, regulations state that you must carry out all human waste with you.

Washing

It is important to protect water sources, and care needs to be taken when washing in the outdoors. The best way to do this is to avoid using any kind of soap. In other words, just use water (ideally hot) and a bit of elbow grease. Biodegradable soaps, whilst they biodegrade over a period of time, can still have an adverse impact on the environment.

INFO

The Countryside Code

- Be safe, plan ahead and follow any signs.
- Leave gates and property as you find them.
- Protect plants and animals, and take your litter home.
- Keep dogs under close control.
- Consider other people.

Visit **http://www.naturalengland.org.uk/ourwork/enjoying/countrysidecode** for more information.

Après Walk

“In every walk with nature one receives far more than he seeks.”

John Muir
Naturalist and conservationist (1838—1914)

Chapter 12

Après Walk

It's not over 'til the fat lady sings

Picture the scene. Your day's walk is coming to an end, and one thing is dominating your thoughts – where on earth did I leave my car? In the eagerness to start your walk, it is easy to forget to establish exactly where you left your vehicle, and where it is in relation to the end of the walk.

Work this out before you set off, to prevent frayed tempers at the end of the day, when all you really want to do is get your boots off. Before you start your walk, double check the location of your car and mark its position on your map, or note it down in some other way. The same applies if you have travelled by public transport. Note the location of your nearest bus-stop.

Stretching after your walk

Gentle stretching after your walk helps loosen up your muscles and promotes recovery. Focus on calf, thigh and back stretches. Ease into each stretch without bouncing or forcing, and hold for twenty seconds. Hold onto something, or someone, for support.

Upper calf stretch

Stand facing a wall and place your hands on it, with your arms straight for support. Push one leg out behind you, keeping it straight, whilst keeping your front leg slightly bent. Press the heel of your back foot flat to the floor. You should feel the stretch in your upper calf.

Lower calf stretch

Lean forward and place both hands on one of your knees for support. Keep your supporting leg slightly bent. Bring one foot forward, with your knee slightly bent. Lift the toes of the front foot to stretch the muscle under the calf.

Quadriceps (front of upper leg)

Hold onto a wall for support. With one hand, grasp your foot and pull it up behind you, towards your buttocks. Use the hand opposite to the leg you want to stretch. Feel the stretch on the front of your upper leg.

Back Stretch

Clasp your hands together. Push your chin towards your chest and push your arms out in front of you. Feel the stretch of your neck and upper back. You can intensify the stretch by leaning forward slightly.

Foot massage

After your walk, treat your feet by massaging foot powder into them. This warms, dries, and relaxes them. You will feel the benefit immediately. Antifungicidal powders also prevent and treat fungal infections. Make it a must-do ritual after each walk.

TOP T!P

To ease aching feet, wrap a cold drinks can in a plastic bag, place it on the floor, then roll over it with the base of your bare foot.

Warm, dry clothes

Having warm, dry clothes to change into directly after your walk feels good and helps keep you warm. If you have driven to your location, leave a spare set of clothes waiting for you in your car. If not, either carry a lightweight set with you, or at the very least, take a fresh pair of socks with you to change into (it still feels good).

Talk the walk

Part of the fun of walking is relaxing with your companions afterwards. An end of walk drink or meal is a rewarding way to finish off your day, and to relive the day's adventures. It's an opportunity to meet other walkers, make new friends, and gain useful information about walking routes, campsites and other local facilities.

Photography

Taking photographs during your walks is a great way of recording your day out in the countryside. It is also a good way of remembering routes, should you wish to revisit them, or to recommend them to friends.

Compact digital cameras are lightweight, and photographs can be easily printed, emailed and stored on your PC. There are a number of digital cameras that are water resistant, which is useful, as it is easy to get cameras wet in the rain. It is good sense to protect your camera by carrying it inside a plastic bag, or small dry bag, to prevent it from getting damaged.

You can create online albums, which you can share with friends and family. You can also upload images and produce photo books, and even add your photographs to T-shirts, mugs and calendars. These can be fun ways of remembering your walking adventures and experiences.

Caring for your boots

Cleaning

Remove any mud from your boots by banging them together, or by using a brush and a little water.

Drying

Wet boots should have their laces and insoles removed, then be stuffed with rolled-up newspaper – before being left to dry naturally. Replace the newspaper once or twice. Avoid placing boots in unnaturally hot areas, as this may make them dry too quickly and crack.

Treating

Once dry, apply leather/fabric treatment as per the manufacturer's instructions. This helps prevent your boots from cracking and makes them easier to clean in the future.

Looking after your waterproofs

Waterproof clothing lasts longer and performs better if you take care of it. Allow waterproofs to dry naturally. Periodically clean and re-waterproof them, by following the manufacturer's instructions and using the products they recommend.

Care of equipment

General advice

- Allow any wet items to dry naturally.
- Open-up and lay out tents and rucksacks to prevent them from becoming mouldy.
- Don't store sleeping bags and down jackets compressed into stuff sacks – this will reduce their insulating qualities.
- Brush off mud and dirt once the items are dry.
- Make sure electronic devices are thoroughly dry. Don't store them for long periods with their batteries installed.
- Dry small items, such as Swiss Army knives and compasses.

- Thoroughly clean the inside of drinking vessels and their drinking tubes.
- Store your equipment in a clean, dry, well-vented area.

TOP T!P

If you wear your waterproofs regularly, clean and re-waterproof them every six months. Always use a good quality proprietary brand of re-waterproofing spray or liquid, and follow the instructions to the letter.

Walk journal

Many people keep a journal to log their outdoor walks. It's a good way to remember them. Recording the time taken and the distance covered helps you plan future walks, with far greater accuracy and efficiency.

Some people set out to 'collect' hill and mountain tops. Having a target keeps them motivated. Climbing all the 'Wainwrights' (the 214 fells described in A. Wainwright's seven-volume *Pictorial Guide to the Lakeland Fells*) or 'Munros' (Scottish mountains with a height over 3,000 feet) has become peak-bagging quests for many people.

Blog

A modern development of the journal is the 'blog' – or 'weblog'. These are simplified websites that are used as online journals, where people share their thoughts and experiences with the world. They are free and easy to set up, and photographs can be uploaded onto them. They are enjoyable to set up and to keep updated.

Blogs have become popular with walkers, and they can be a useful source of information about walking areas. See **www.blogger.com**

Keeping fit between walks

If you aim to tackle more challenging routes, you may need to increase the amount of exercise you do. If it's not possible to fit more walking into your schedule, or you want to add some variety into your exercise routine, try other forms of exercise. Exercises that develop your aerobic capacity and leg strength are best, but a good all round fitness regime prevents boredom and avoids injury. Talk to a fitness trainer, who can help you put together a suitable training plan.

Learn more, see more

Learn more about the history of the areas in which you intend to walk. It can be fascinating and will add interest to your outings. Improving your knowledge of the natural world will also enhance your walks. Things that you previously passed by, and didn't notice, suddenly become enthralling.

Walking is for everyone!

Walking enriches our lives and improves our health, fitness and mental well-being. By tailoring walks to our capabilities, almost everyone can enjoy it. Whether it's a short stroll or a challenging trek – it's good for us. By putting on our boots and going for a walk, we can escape from the rat-race and discover new places. Where will your feet take you?

Rights of Way and Access Symbols

The information here relates to 1:25,000 OS Maps

- Footpath
- Bridleway
- Byway open to all traffic
- Restricted byway (not for use by mechanically propelled vehicles)

Rights of way are liable to change and may not be clearly defined on the ground. Please check with the relevant local authority for the latest information. Rights of way are not shown on maps of Scotland.

Other Public Access

Other routes with public access (not normally shown in urban areas)
The exact nature of the rights on these routes and the existence of any restrictions may be checked with the local highway authority. Alignments are based on the best information available.

National Trail / Long Distance Route — Recreational Route

Permissive footpath
Permissive bridleway

Footpaths and bridleways along which landowners have permitted public use but which are not rights of way. The agreement may be withdrawn.

Traffic-free cycle route

1 National cycle network route number – traffic free

1 National cycle network route number – on road

Scotland

In Scotland, everyone has access rights in law* over most land and inland water, provided access is exercised responsibly. This includes walking, cycling, horse-riding and water access, for recreational and educational purposes, and for crossing land or water. Access rights do not apply to motorised activities, hunting, shooting or fishing, nor if your dog is not under proper control. The Scottish Outdoor Access Code is the reference point for responsible behaviour, and can be obtained at www.outdooraccess-scotland.com or by phoning your local Scottish Natural Heritage office. *Land Reform (Scotland) Act 2003

National Trust for Scotland, always open / limited opening – observe local signs

Forestry Commission Land / Woodland Trust Land

England & Scotland

DANGER AREA

Firing and test ranges in the area. Danger! Observe warning notices. Visit www.access.mod.uk for information.

Access Land

Access land boundary and tint

Access land in woodland area

Access information point

MANAGED ACCESS

Access permitted within managed controls for example, local byelaws. Visit www.access.mod.uk for information.

England

Portrayal of access land on a map is intended as a guide to land which is normally available for access on foot, for example access land created under the Countryside and Rights of Way Act 2000, and land managed by the National Trust, Forestry Commission and Woodland Trust. Access for other activities may also exist. Some restrictions will apply; some land will be excluded from open access rights. The depiction of rights of access does not imply or express any warranty as to its accuracy or completeness. Observe local signs and follow the Countryside Code. Visit www.naturalengland.org.uk/ourwork/enjoying/countrysidecode for up-to-date information.

Charts & Planners

Route Planner		Date	Group members Telephone nos.	Local accommodation Start Point				Start time Finish time (Est.)	
Leg	*From*	*To*	*Leg description*	*Direction / bearing*	*Distance in metres / kilometres*	*Metres of ascent*	*Estimated time taken*	*Add rest stops*	*Est. time of arrival*
1									
2									
3									
4									
5									
6									
7									
Totals									
Weather report			Escape route			Copy of planner left with Name Telephone no.			

Timing charts

Distance in metres	Time taken based on walking speed of 4 kph
100	
200	
400	
600	
800	
1 kilometre	
2 kilometres	
4 kilometres	

Additional time for ascent

Metres of ascent	100	200	400	600	800	1000
Extra time to be added						

Pacing chart

Add your own number of paces for each distance for flat ground and steeper terrain.

Terrain	100 m	75 m	50 m	25 m
Level terrain				
Steep terrain				

Beaufort Scale of Wind Speeds

Force	Wind Speed		Description	Effects on Land and at Sea
	mph	km/hr		
0	<1	<1	Calm	Still, calm air, smoke will rise vertically. Water is mirror-like.
1	1–3	1–5	Light Air	Rising smoke drifts, wind vane is inactive. Small ripples appear on water surface.
2	4–7	6–11	Light Breeze	Leaves rustle, can feel wind on your face, wind vanes begin to move. Small wavelets develop, crests are glassy.
3	8–12	12–19	Gentle Breeze	Leaves and small twigs move, light weight flags extend. Large wavelets, crests start to break, some whitecaps.
4	13–18	20–28	Moderate Breeze	Small branches move, raises dust, leaves and paper. Small waves develop, becoming longer, whitecaps.
5	19–24	29–38	Fresh Breeze	Small trees sway. White crested wavelets (whitecaps) form, some spray.
6	25–31	39–49	Strong Breeze	Large tree branches move, telephone wires begin to "whistle", umbrellas are difficult to keep under control. Larger waves form, whitecaps prevalent, spray.
7	32–38	50–61	Moderate or Near Gale	Large trees sway, becoming difficult to walk. Larger waves develop, white foam from breaking waves begins to be blown.
8	39–46	62–74	Gale or Fresh Gale	Twigs and small branches are broken from trees, walking is difficult. Moderately large waves with blown foam.
9	47–54	75–88	Strong Gale	Slight damage occurs to buildings, shingles are blown off of roofs. High waves (6 metres), rolling seas, dense foam, Blowing spray reduces visibility.
10	55–63	89–102	Whole Gale or Storm	Trees are broken or uprooted, building damage is considerable. Large waves (6-9 metres), overhanging crests, sea becomes white with foam, heavy rolling, reduced visibility.

11	64–72	103–117	Violent Storm	Extensive, widespread damage. Large waves (9-14 metres), white foam, visibility further reduced.
12	73+	118+	Hurricane	Extreme destruction, devastation. Large waves over 14 metres, air filled with foam, sea white with foam and driving spray, little visibility.

Sunrise and Sunset Table

	Glasgow, Scotland, UK		London, England, UK	
Month	sunrise	sunset	sunrise	sunset
January	08:38	16:15	08:00	16:20
February	07:43	17:20	07:16	17:14
March	06:31	18:21	06:14	18:06
April	06:11	20:24	06:04	19:58
May	05:04	21:24	05:08	20:46
June	04:31	22:04	04:43	21:20
July	04:53	21:52	05:01	21:11
August	05:49	20:52	05:46	20:22
September	06:49	19:34	06:36	19:14
October	07:49	18:16	07:25	18:06
November	07:54	16:09	07:19	16:11
December	08:42	15:43	08:00	15:52

Note: Sunrise is when the upper part of the sun becomes visible over the horizon. Sunset is when the sun is about to disappear below the horizon.

Sunrise and sunset times are based on the 15th day of each month. These are based on ideal conditions, clear visibility, and the viewer being located at the same altitude as a flat horizon, with no mountains obscuring the view.

Useful Websites

Walking for Health: www.wfh.naturalengland.org.uk

Ramblers Association: www.ramblers.org.uk

Long Distance Walkers Association: www.ldwa.org.uk

NHS Choices: www.nhs.uk/Livewell

Ordnance Survey Maps: www.ordnancesurvey.co.uk

Natural England: www.naturalengland.gov.uk

Scottish access advice: www.snh.org.uk/hillphones

Weather reports: www.metoffice.gov.uk

Weather reports: www.metcheck.com

Sunrise and sunset times: www.timeanddate.com

Scottish avalanche information: www.sais.gov.uk

First aid advice: www.nhsdirect.nhs.uk

Mountain Rescue: www.mountain.rescue.org.uk

Outdoor advice Scotland: www.outdooraccess-scotland.com

Footpath repairs and advice: www.fixthefells.co.uk

National Trust: www.nationaltrust.org.uk

Blogging: www.blogger.com

Photography advice: www.better-photos.co.uk

Picture Credits

Cover, Title, P13, P80–81 © A-Digit/iStockphoto, P4 © ROBERTO CAUCINO/iStockphoto, P8 © Ljupco Smokovski/Fotolia, P12 © Martinmark/Dreamstime, P15 © Carmentianya/Dreamstime, P18 © Ben Blankenburg/iStockphoto, P25 © Pro777/Dreamstime, P28 © skankimages/Fotolia, P33 © flucas/Fotolia, P47 © Martin Kawalski/iStockphoto, P53 © Wojciech Zwierzynski/iStockphoto, P54 © Olga Lyubkin/Fotolia, P62 © AVAVA/Fotolia, P67 © Martinmark/Dreamstime, P68 © Yuri Arcurs/Fotolia, P73 © Werg/Dreamstime, P79 © Vichaya Kiatying-angsulee/Dreamstime, P82 © LE image/Fotolia, P89 © Gynane/Dreamstime, P91 © Susan H. Smith/iStockphoto, P97 © Terrance Emerson/iStockphoto, P98 © ville ahonen/Fotolia, P120 © Greg Epperson/Dreamstime, P125 © Alberto Pomares/iStockphoto, P130 © Constantin Opris/Dreamstime, P139 © Reinhardt/Dreamstime, P146 © Mark S. Elliott/Author, P148 © Jakub Cejpek/Dreamstime, P155 © Jon Helgason/iStockphoto, P158 © Hans Chris/iStockphoto, P162 © Peterguess/Dreamstime, P167 © Kirill Medvedev/Dreamstime, P172 © Marek Surkala/Fotolia, P188–189 © Martinmark/Dreamstime.

Index